Key Concepts in
aching Primary
Mathematics

The SAGE Key Concepts series provides students with accessible and authoritative knowledge of the essential topics in a variety of disciplines. Cross referenced throughout, the format encourages critical evaluation through understanding. Written by experienced and respected academics, the books are indispensable study aids and guides to comprehension.

DEREK HAYLOCK WITH FIONA THANGATA

Key Concepts in
Teaching Primary
Mathematics

SAGE Publications
Los Angeles • London • New Delhi • Singapore

First published 2007

 SAGE Publications Ltd
1 Oliver's Yard
55 City Road
London EC1Y 1SP

SAGE Publications Inc.
2455 Teller Road
Thousand Oaks, California 91320

SAGE Publications India Pvt Ltd
B 1/I 1 Mohan Cooperative Industrial Area
Mathura Road, New Delhi 110 044
India

SAGE Publications Asia-Pacific Pte Ltd
33 Pekin Street #02-01
Far East Square
Singapore 048763

Library of Congress Control Number: 2007925061

British Library Cataloguing in Publication data

A catalogue record for this book is available from the
British Library

ISBN 978-1-4129-3409-1
ISBN 978-1-4129-3410-7 (pbk)

Typeset by C&M Digitals (P) Ltd, Chennai, India
Printed in Great Britain by The Cromwell Press, Trowbridge, Wiltshire
Printed on paper from sustainable resources

contents

contents

v

the authors

Dr Derek Haylock is an education consultant and author, working particularly in the field of mathematics education. He is a Senior Fellow in Education at the University of East Anglia, Norwich, where he taught for over 20 years, undertook research in mathematics education and headed up the primary initial teacher training. He has had published a number of single-authored, co-authored and edited books, and chapters in books. His book *Mathematics Explained for Primary Teachers* has been a leader in the field for many years, with a third edition published in 2006.

Dr Fiona Thangata is a Lecturer in Mathematics Education at the University of East Anglia, Norwich, where she teaches on the primary Postgraduate Certificate of Education (PGCE). She has contributed a number of articles to journals and chapters in books. She has worked in England, Scotland, Namibia and the USA as a classroom teacher, curriculum developer, in-service provider and teacher trainer.

Introduction

What are the most important concepts related to teaching and learning that a teacher of mathematics in a primary school should know something about? That was the question we had before us in setting out to write this book. Our task was to come up with 40 to 50 such key concepts, and then to provide a definition, some explanation and discussion of each concept, some practical examples related to the classroom, and suggestions for further reading. This we have done, although we must admit that we have interpreted the word 'concept' rather more loosely than we would have allowed one of our students to get away with! There are essentially four kinds of 'concepts' included in this book:

- key teaching skills for primary mathematics teachers;
- key issues in the primary mathematics curriculum;
- key ways in which pupils in primary schools learn mathematics;
- key ways in which primary pupils learn to reason mathematically.

It will be helpful for the reader to be aware of two kinds of concepts that are not included. First, the entries in this book do not include purely mathematical concepts, like 'equilateral triangle' or 'prime number'. For explanation of such mathematical concepts the reader is referred to *Mathematics Explained for Primary Teachers* 3rd edition (Haylock, 2006). Second, we have limited ourselves to concepts about teaching and learning where we feel there is something distinctive or significant to say in relation to mathematics in primary schools. So, for example, although skills in managing pupil behaviour are absolutely essential for being an effective teacher of mathematics, there is nothing special to say about this topic in mathematics that would not apply to any subject. So, the teaching skills that are included, such as explanation, questioning and differentiation, are those where we judge that there is something significant to say from the perspective of the mathematics educator.

In 2007, the primary school curriculum in England is at an interesting stage of development. The National Curriculum (DfEE, 1999a) is still the statutory document that determines what should be taught in schools. However, in practice, in the early years of the current millennium, the most influential document in relation to teaching mathematics in primary schools has been the framework of the National Numeracy Strategy (DfEE, 1999b). This framework has made a significant impact on practice in primary schools, much of it good, but with a number of shortcomings emerging during the course of its implementation. The government has initiated a review of the Primary Strategy and many of the shortcomings have been addressed (DfES, 2006a, 2006b; and the website, www.standards.dfes.gov.uk/primary). We have therefore done our best to set our discussion of concepts that relate to curriculum issues – such as numeracy, cross-curricular mathematics, and using and applying mathematics – into the context of all three of the National Curriculum, the National Numeracy Strategy and the revised Primary Strategy.

The entries in this book are arranged alphabetically, rather than thematically, so they can be read and referred to in any order. However, for each entry we have indicated up to four related entries that provide further information on some of the ideas or issues raised in the topic being considered.

Aims of Mathematics Teaching

DEFINITION

The aims of teaching mathematics are those long-term purposes that together constitute the justification for the subject having such a prominent place in the school curriculum. They are the answer to the question: why teach mathematics? The aims of mathematics teaching can be categorized under five headings: utilitarian, application, transferable skills, aesthetic and epistemological.

EXPLANATION AND DISCUSSION

The mathematics section of the National Curriculum for England begins with a statement that embraces these five categories of aims for teaching this subject:

> Mathematics equips pupils with a uniquely powerful set of tools to understand and change the world. These tools include logical reasoning, problem-solving skills, and the ability to think in abstract ways. Mathematics is important in everyday life, many forms of employment, science and technology, medicine, the economy, the environment and development, and in public decision-making. Different cultures have contributed to the development and application of mathematics. Today, the subject transcends human boundaries and its importance is universally recognised. Mathematics is a creative discipline. It can stimulate moments of pleasure and wonder when a pupil solves a problem for the first time, discovers a more elegant solution to that problem, or suddenly sees hidden connections. (DfEE, 1999a: 60)

Utilitarian

The utilitarian aims for teaching mathematics are related to numeracy, which is understood as equipping the individual to cope with the mathematical demands of everyday life and the basic needs of most forms of employment. Most forms of employment require a basic level of numeracy: confidence with number, measurement, manipulating shapes, organizing space, handling money, recording numerical information, handling data in simple graphical form, and so on. The fact that 'mathematics is important in everyday life' and in 'many forms of employment', as stated in the National Curriculum quotation above, is one of the main rationales for the place of mathematics as a core subject in the curriculum: 'This fact in itself could be thought to provide a sufficient reason for teaching mathematics' (Cockcroft, 1982: para. 1). An aim such as 'preparing pupils not only for the world of work, but for active citizenship and responsibilities as members of households' (Goulding, 1997: 128) is relevant to all pupils, whatever their future courses of study or forms of employment.

Application

A frequently cited aim for teaching mathematics is that of equipping pupils with the knowledge and skills that they will require to function effectively in a range of other subjects in the curriculum. The National Curriculum quotation above, for example, mentions the subject's importance in science and technology, medicine, economics, and so on. Goulding (1997: 129) identifies the need for data-handling skills in history and biology; for skills in measurement, ratio and scale in art, technology, science and geography; and for algebraic skills in science. In his influential book on mathematics as an educational task, Freudenthal (1973: 67), while recognizing the importance of application in mathematics, introduces a realistic note of caution: 'All of us understand that mathematics admits of numerous applications and that more pupils than ever will have to apply mathematics. We would be fortunate if we could tell of each of them which mathematical concepts and techniques he [or she] would need in the future.'

Transferable skills

An aim of mathematics teaching might be to develop through this subject particular kinds of thinking skills, which, it is assumed, will develop pupils' general intellectual capacity and enable them to apply the kinds of reasoning they use in a mathematical context in a range of circumstances and problem-solving situations. The National Curriculum quotation above reflects this kind of aim, mentioning, for example, the potential contribution of mathematics to the development of logical reasoning, problem solving and abstract thinking. There has been considerable interest in British primary education in recent years in the development of 'thinking skills'. What has not been addressed with sufficient rigour is the question of the educational conditions under which thinking skills developed in one context, such as mathematics, might or might not be transferable more generally. It is certainly true that doing mathematics at a certain level requires particular kinds of logical thinking, such as reasoning analytically, arguing deductively, and the awareness of the distinction between a conjecture and a proven generalization, for example. These are powerful kinds of thinking that are important in many spheres of life. But the question is whether or not they transfer. Does learning to think logically and analytically in mathematics make an individual more logical and analytical in their approach to human relationships, problem solving in the workplace, personal finances and political debate?

Aesthetic

The National Curriculum quotation above emphasizes the pleasure and wonder that can be experienced by pupils engaging with mathematics. This introduces the possibility of an aesthetic aim in teaching the subject, which would justify mathematics in the same terms as we would justify the teaching of music, literature or art: here is a potential source of human aesthetic experience and it is our responsibility to open up this world of delight and beauty to our pupils! Freudenthal (1973: 69) suggests that 'for quite a few it is the aim of mathematics teaching to introduce children into a system of mathematics, a system that irradiates undeniably aesthetic charm … ' – but again he introduces a note of caution – 'which, however, cannot be apprehended by people who have no profound knowledge of mathematics'.

Epistemological

Discussion of aesthetic aims in mathematics teaching raises then the question as to whether all such aims are realistic and relevant for all pupils. This is a particularly pertinent question in relation to our fifth category, epistemological aims. These would be aims related to the nature of knowledge. Mathematics is a distinctive and universal field of human knowledge, which, as the National Curriculum quotation recognizes, has drawn on different cultures and centuries of human endeavour. One definition of an educated person would be someone who has a grasp of all the major fields of knowledge, so that initiation into the academic discipline of mathematics is as essential as understanding the notion of historical evidence or the nature of scientific theory. Pupils therefore must be introduced to mathematics and the ways in which mathematicians reason. This is not to say that we pretend that we are training all pupils to be potential mathematicians.

> One thing can be predicted with near certainty, that is, that [the average pupil] probably will not become a mathematician … Again and again we should stress this one point that is so easily forgotten: that besides the future mathematician a great many others must learn mathematics, that those who finally apply a relatively sophisticated mathematics are a minority among those who will apply mathematics at all, and that even those who will never apply mathematics should learn mathematics because they need it as one aspect of their being human beings. (Freudenthal, 1973: 68–9)

PRACTICAL EXAMPLES

Discussion like this will seem a long way from the reality of the primary classroom on a Monday morning when a teacher struggles to get pupils to deal correctly with a zero in the first number in a subtraction. Teachers operate on the basis of medium-term goals in designing their schemes of work and short-term goals in their daily lesson plans. But this is not to say that such aims as those categorized above are irrelevant. It is at the level of preparing a school's curriculum policy statement for mathematics that such considerations will come into play. Below are examples of statements of aims for teaching mathematics in a primary school, reflecting the five categories described above, that might appear in such a curriculum policy statement. When such aims have been adopted as school policy, those who monitor and evaluate a school's work would expect to see evidence in medium-term plans and in the practice within actual lessons that the experience of pupils is being shaped to promote these longer-term purposes.

- To lay the foundation for the basic mathematical skills and knowledge that pupils will need to deal confidently with the numerical situations they will encounter in their normal, everyday life, now and in the future as adults in employment and within society.

- To equip the pupils with mathematical skills and knowledge that they will need to progress in other subjects within the school curriculum and to enable them to recognize the important role of mathematics in other areas of learning.
- To develop the pupils' ability within mathematics to think logically, to explain their reasoning, to analyse, to apply strategies to solve problems, to recognize pattern, to generalize concepts and principles.
- To promote a positive attitude towards the subject, by ensuring that mathematical experience is enjoyable, stimulating, creative and fascinating.
- To promote awareness of some of the contributions of various cultures to the body of mathematical knowledge.

FURTHER READING

For a different conception of the aims of mathematics teaching read a chapter entitled 'Why teach mathematics?' by Paul Ernest (in White and Bramall, 2000). Ernest's arguments are engaging and characteristically challenging. Other chapters in the same book explore various ideas related to why pupils should learn mathematics.

RELATED ENTRIES

Cross-curricular mathematics. Deductive and inductive reasoning. Numeracy. Using and applying mathematics.

Algorithm

DEFINITION

An algorithm is a standard procedure that involves a number of steps, which, if followed correctly, can be relied upon to lead to the solution of a particular kind of problem. In primary mathematics the word is usually used to refer to a standard written procedure for carrying out a calculation with multidigit numbers, such as the method of decomposition for subtraction or the method of long multiplication.

EXPLANATION AND DISCUSSION

Although there are many informal methods available to them, there are clearly some advantages for pupils in mastering some formal algorithms for the calculations they might be expected to be able to do without a calculator before they leave primary school, such as 4357 + 946, 805 − 436, 64 × 38 and 648 ÷ 24. The main argument put forward in favour of teaching these algorithms is that pupils will thereby always have a method for any calculation they are faced with, which can be relied on to work in every case, and which they can use when an appropriate informal method is not immediately available to them. In using an algorithm, the procedure to be followed is usually the same, regardless of the numbers involved. An argument against would be that a huge proportion of the teaching time available is being devoted to tasks that in practice will be done on a cheap calculator, with much greater efficiency. Askew (2001: 113) expresses the view that although the procedure adopted by most adults for calculations such as those above would be to reach for a calculator, it is for 'political rather than educational reasons' that paper-and-pencil procedures continue to be dominant in the school curriculum.

Pupils make a wide range of errors in carrying out algorithmic procedures for calculations. Many of these are associated with the vertical layout used in most algorithms – for example, in subtraction by decomposition, when one number is written directly below the other. Fuson (2004) reports that many research studies indicate that children do not show quantity understandings of the digits when they are manipulating multidigit numbers. So, for example, when 268 is written underneath 387 in order to add them, children see the 268 as 'two six eight' and lose the sense that the 2 represents 200 and the 6 represents 60, and so on. Consequently, some children will write down an answer such as 51415 for this addition (2 + 3 = 5, 6 + 8 = 14, and 8 + 7 = 15). It appears that the vertical format encourages pupils to treat the two 3-digit numbers as two sets of three separate numbers to be combined in some way.

Learning an algorithmic procedure can encourage pupils to regard a formal written calculation simply as a question of having to remember which particular recipe you use for this operation when the numbers are arranged on the paper in this particular way. In other words, they can easily slip into relying upon rote learning rather than on understanding. A common error in subtraction occurs when one of the digits in the smaller number is a zero (for example, 724 – 302) and pupils attempt to apply inappropriately the procedure for decomposition that is required when there is a zero in the top number (Resnick, 1982).

A further problem is when pupils pick up – possibly from parents or from teachers – the idea that the algorithm is the 'proper' way to do a particular type of calculation and then use it regardless of the numbers involved. For example, a 9-year-old might get in a muddle trying to subtract 198 from 202 by using the decomposition algorithm, when they could easily do this mentally by counting on from 198. One of the authors gave some 11-year-olds some multiplications with 2-digit numbers. The question that most of them got wrong was 20 × 10. Even though they admitted afterwards that they knew the answer was 200, they had tried to apply the long multiplication algorithm they had been taught (and got in a muddle with all the zeros) because they thought that this was what was expected of them.

It is important therefore that, when teaching an algorithm, primary school teachers do not send out the message to their pupils that this is the proper way to do this kind of calculation and that the algorithm now replaces all those mental and informal strategies they have been developing.

The National Curriculum for England and Wales (DfEE, 1999a) did not actually prescribe the teaching of any particular algorithms for calculations to pupils in primary schools. However, the Numeracy Strategy (DfEE, 1999b), with all its emphasis on the importance of mental and informal methods, nevertheless expected pupils by the age of 9 years to have developed 'an efficient method that can be applied generally' for addition and subtraction, and provided examples using the standard layout for column addition (p. 48) and subtraction by decomposition (p. 50). The revised National Strategy for primary schools in England is markedly more prescriptive about which algorithms should be taught in primary schools, seeking to 'promote wider and more consistent use of what are commonly known as "standard" written methods ...' (DfES, 2006a: 3).

PRACTICAL EXAMPLES

The two practical suggestions below are based on the assumption that algorithms should be taught with understanding.

Making connections

To counteract the tendency to learn algorithms by rote, primary teachers have to spend time helping pupils to understand the procedures. This usually involves making strong connections between the manipulation of the symbols, the associated language and some form of concrete materials or images (Haylock, 2006. ch. 6). For example, to make sense of the decomposition algorithm for 435 – 269, pupils might use 4 pound coins to represent the 4 hundreds in 435, 3 ten-pence coins to represent the 3 tens and 5 penny coins to represent the 5 units (ones). To subtract the 9 units in 269 they have to take away 9 pennies. But there are only 5 of these, so they exchange one of the 3 tens at the bank for 10 pennies. They now have 15 pennies, and can take away 9, leaving 6 pennies. They then have to take away 6 tens … and so on. By the use of appropriate language ('exchange one ten for ten ones') and by making connections between the recording of the calculation and the manipulation of the coins, the teacher promotes understanding of the procedure.

Choice of algorithm

Primary teachers should be aware that there are several algorithms or variations on an algorithm available for each operation. Their choice might be guided by two principles: (a) the extent to which they can help pupils to make sense of the procedure and therefore to apply it with understanding, rather than by rote; (b) whether it is accessible for primary school pupils, in terms of the complexity of the skills required to carry it out. Haylock (2006: 101 – 3) rules out the teaching of the method of long division, for example, on the grounds that the procedure is very difficult to teach with understanding, and that it involves skills that are too complex to be accessible to pupils in this age range. Instead he advocates the use of an ad hoc method of repeated subtraction, supported by an appropriate method of recording. This is also the method for teaching in primary schools advocated by the influential Dutch TAL group (Treffers et al., 2001).

Grid method for multiplication

Many primary school teachers in England have adopted the 'grid method' for multiplication because it is a procedure that is more understandable and more accessible than the more compact traditional method of long multiplication. Although the Numeracy Strategy

```
        64
      × 38
      1920    (64 × 30)
       512    (64 × 8)
      2432    (64 × 38)
```

	60	4
30	1800	120
8	480	32

2280 + 152 = 2432

Figure 1 *Comparing the long multiplication algorithm and the grid method for 64 × 38*

(DfEE, 1999b: 67) included this approach to multiplication as an informal method, it qualifies in every respect as an algorithm. Figure 1 compares the two methods for the calculation of 64 × 38. The condensed form of the traditional long multiplication method is achieved by reducing the calculation to three steps, the first two of which are demanding in their own right: 64 × 30, 64 × 8, and then the addition of these two results. The less compact grid method requires more, but easier, steps: 60 × 30, 60 × 8, 4 × 30, 4 × 8, followed by the addition of these four results. The layout of the calculation can also be connected with the image of a rectangular field, 64 units by 38 units, where the area is to be calculated by dividing it up into four smaller fields, to promote greater understanding of the procedure. The revised National Strategy for primary schools (DfES, 2006a: 48–50) prescribes the teaching of the grid method, but presents it as a stage in the development of the compact long multiplication algorithm, rather than as an efficient and acceptable algorithm in its own right.

FURTHER READING

Highly recommended is the chapter entitled 'Column calculation and algorithms', by Treffers et al. for the TAL project in The Netherlands (in van den Heuvel-Panhuizen, 2001). Askew, in a chapter entitled 'Policy, practices and principles in teaching numeracy': what makes a difference?' (in Gates, 2001), provides a helpful analysis of the key differences between strategic (informal) and procedural (algorithmic) methods of calculation. Fuson, in a chapter entitled 'Pre-K to Grade 2 goals and standards' (in Clements and Sarama, 2004) provides an interesting US perspective on accessible algorithms for addition and subtraction for pupils up to age 7 years. See also the guidance provided in the

algorithm

11

National Strategy for primary schools (DfES, 2006a), together with its associated website (www.standards.dfes.gov.uk/primary/mathematics).

RELATED ENTRIES

Informal calculation method. Mental calculation. Rote learning. Skill learning.

Anxiety About Mathematics

DEFINITION

Anxiety can be defined as a 'complex emotional response, often unconscious in origin, with fear or dread as its most notable characteristic' (Page and Thomas, 1979). This definition describes the condition of anxiety about mathematics that inhibits the ability of some individuals to achieve their potential in this subject – with the experience of learning and assessment of mathematics in a classroom as both the source of the emotional response and the object of the fear or dread.

EXPLANATION AND DISCUSSION

It is quite normal for some pupils to be anxious to do their best in school and to worry about tests and getting their work wrong. However, there is clearly such a phenomenon as 'mathematics anxiety', an unhelpful level and quality of anxiety about this particular subject, which interferes with the individual's ability to learn and to do their best. Haylock (1986) found that 26 per cent of pupils aged 10 to 11 years who were regarded by their teachers as being low attainers in mathematics were judged to show an abnormal level of anxiety towards the subject. This was a factor associated significantly more often with low-attaining girls than with low-attaining boys. Ford et al. (2005) report that by the age of 10 years some pupils describe the same kinds of feelings as those of the typical adult who suffers from mathematics anxiety. Their findings support the view that mathematics anxiety interferes with the working memory that we need to do calculations, so that people who are perfectly competent at the subject perform less well than they could do otherwise. The anxious, intrusive thoughts generated by the mathematical task compete for limited memory space and disrupt the mathematical processes.

Ashcraft and Kirk (2001) propose that anxiety about mathematics worsens performance in two ways. First, it leads to avoidance, which leads to lower competence. Second, it temporarily inhibits working memory capacity, possibly by failure to inhibit attention to intrusive thoughts. They suggest that their findings might explain why the most effective interventions for mathematics anxiety are the cognitive-behavioural ones. So teachers should help anxious pupils to learn to manage the anxiety itself. Ashcraft and Kirk argue that mathematics anxiety is learned, and therefore it can be unlearned and overcome.

Anxiety about mathematics is exhibited in a number of ways, such as those given below.

- The pupil panics when faced with a mathematics task and is unable to think clearly and to recall things that they know and can do.
- The pupil has a feeling of fear when faced with a mathematical task and an excessive worry about getting answers wrong.
- The pupil develops a conviction that they cannot do this subject and expects to do badly in any kind of mathematics assessment.
- Because they are convinced they cannot understand, the pupil resorts to a rote-learning mode, relying on memorization of rules and recipes, rather than on understanding.

This anxiety may have its source in the interaction between the pupil's experience in the classroom and their personality. Some pupils are not as good at dealing with mistakes and failure than others. It is an unfortunate aspect of school mathematics that we are required to generate responses that will be judged to be absolutely correct or absolutely wrong, in a way that distinguishes the experience of learning this subject from that of others in the school curriculum.

Parents and, even, primary school teachers themselves can have significant levels of anxiety about mathematics and may often pass on their own anxiety to the children (Burnett and Wichman, 1997). Haylock (2006: 3–4) reports that many trainees start primary teacher training courses with considerable anxiety about having to teach mathematics and that this stems from their own experience of learning the subject at school. When the trainees spoke about their memories of mathematics classrooms their comments contained references to fear, horror, terror and nightmares.

PRACTICAL EXAMPLES

In the primary classroom, teachers must be alert to the possibility of fostering anxiety towards mathematics in their pupils by the kind of teaching style they adopt and the attitudes they may communicate. Some practical ways in which teachers can avoid fostering anxiety in mathematics are given below.

- Be sensitive to individual pupils who seem unhelpfully anxious; set targets for reducing this anxiety through encouragement, reassurance and by sympathetically avoiding putting such pupils under unnecessary pressure; for example, do not expect them to answer questions or demonstrate mathematical procedures in public.
- Do not limit mathematical experiences to tasks that are right or wrong.
- In planning tasks for pupils, ensure an appropriate balance between challenge and success. Pupils respond to challenge, but too little success and the repeated experience of failure is likely to foster low self-esteem and anxiety.
- Make sure that the provision of correct answers is not the only thing for which pupils get rewarded in mathematics lessons. Give marks, encouragement, praise and so on, for having good ideas, for thinking creatively, for having a go, for taking risks, and for process.
- Recognize that some pupils need more thinking time than others, so do not put too much emphasis on doing mathematics quickly or expecting children to provide answers to questions instantly.
- Make mathematics enjoyable for pupils, so they want to participate and are less likely to be inhibited.
- Communicate positive attitudes to mathematics and teach the subject with enthusiasm, a sense of humour and fun, showing pupils that you enjoy it and value it.
- Develop a classroom ethos in which pupils know that the teacher welcomes their questions and wants to know if they do not understand.

- When giving pupils any kind of assessment task, emphasize that the main purpose is to help you find out how well you have been teaching them and to teach them better in the future.
- In planning mathematics teaching, set goals for emotional as well as cognitive development. From time to time give pupils opportunities to talk about or write about their feelings towards mathematics.

FURTHER READING

In a very engaging book about the panic induced by mathematics, Buxton (1991) makes the case that emotion must be taken into account in mathematics education as much as cognition. For a summary of research in this area, refer to the chapter by Ashcraft et al. entitled 'On the cognitive consequences of mathematics anxiety' (in Donlan, 1998).

RELATED ENTRIES

Errors. Gender and mathematics. Low attainment. Rote learning.

Assessment for Learning

DEFINITION

'Assessment for learning is the process of seeking and interpreting evidence for use by learners and their teachers to decide where the learners are in their learning, where they need to go and how best to get there' (Assessment Reform Group, 2002, poster downloadable from www.qca.org.uk). Assessment in education refers to any of the many ways in which someone seeks to gain evidence to help them to measure or to make judgements about the quality, quantity or level of a pupil's learning. The emphasis in assessment for learning is on the active engagement of pupils with assessment as an integral component of the learning process.

EXPLANATION AND DISCUSSION

Assessment can be summative or formative. Summative assessment is where the purpose is to make an overall judgement about pupils' learning, mainly for reporting purposes at the end of a period of teaching. Formative assessment is where the purpose is to gather data about the pupils' learning to inform teaching and to promote learning. Assessment of pupils' learning can focus on short-term objectives for one or more lessons, or medium-term goals over a longer period of time. It is much easier to assess short-term, specific objectives, such as: 'By Friday pupils will be able to decide whether or not an integer less than 100 is prime' (see below). It is more difficult to assess medium-term goals couched in less specific language, such as: 'Pupils will develop their ability to use and apply their mathematical knowledge and skills in problem solving and investigations.'

In recent years in England there has been a growing interest in 'assessment for learning'. The emphasis is on assessment *for* learning, rather than assessment *of* learning. This is an approach that emphasizes the role of formative assessment as an effective means for promoting learning. It shifts the focus in formative assessment away from just providing the teacher with information, to help plan their teaching, towards the impact on pupils themselves of their engagement with the process of assessment. The Assessment Reform Group advocates this recognition of how assessment can be part of the process of learning. It involves the pupils themselves in understanding their learning goals and being actively involved in assessing their own progress towards these. This group has provided evidence that when pupils are actively engaged in this process of reviewing their own progress, learning is enhanced and pupils are empowered to take action to improve their own performance (Assessment Reform Group, 1999). Three purposes in assessment for learning would be:

- to provide pupils with feedback on their progress towards agreed learning goals;
- to motivate pupils to do their best work;
- to develop pupils as independent learners with skills of self-assessment.

Mathematics is a subject where this approach might be seen as particularly appropriate, because many of the things that pupils have to learn can be stated with specificity and clarity; so pupils are more likely to understand what they have to learn and to be able to judge whether they have learnt it. However, there is a danger of shifting the focus too much onto those aspects of mathematics that are more easily assessed, such as knowledge and skills, as opposed to higher levels of learning such as understanding, application, problem solving, creativity, and so on. Niss (1993a: 27) warns that 'what is not assessed in education becomes invisible or unimportant'.

PRACTICAL EXAMPLES

Primary school teachers who adopt an assessment for learning approach will:

- share the objectives and goals of their lessons with pupils;
- ensure that pupils understand these objectives and goals;
- make clear to pupils how they will know if they have achieved these objectives and goals;
- give time to discussing the assessment criteria that they will employ, using language the pupils can understand and examples that clarify what counts as success;
- plan assessment opportunities within their lessons, using a variety of means to enable both the teacher and the pupils to gain insights into how the pupils' learning is progressing towards the objectives and goals;
- provide pupils with feedback that highlights what they have achieved and is clear and constructive about their weaknesses and how these might be addressed.

Below is a suggestion as to how some of these principles might work out in practice in a mathematics lesson with a class of 10- to 11-year-olds, using the example of a specific objective given above: 'By Friday pupils will be able to decide whether or not an integer less than 100 is prime.'

At the start of the final lesson of three on prime numbers the objective is displayed to the class, and questioning is used to ensure that pupils understand the key words and concepts involved: integer, less than 100, prime. The class is asked how they might know if they have achieved the objective. A pupil replies that, if the teacher gives them lots of numbers less than 100, they will be able to work out which ones are prime numbers and which ones are not. The teacher agrees and alerts the class to the plan to give them a sheet of ten questions exactly like that, later in the lesson, and that the pupils' target should be to get at least eight of these correct.

After the main teaching part of the lesson and some exploratory group work on determining whether numbers are prime, the assessment task is given to pupils to work through individually. In the final 10 minutes of the lesson, the answers are shared with the class and pupils mark their own responses. The teacher gives time to talk about common difficulties, for example, asking pupils why they think that so many of them wrongly decided that 91 was prime. At the bottom of the sheet each pupil writes a summary of how well they have done, whether they think they have achieved the objective, where they might have had difficulties, and what they have learnt about their learning. The sheets are collected in and, later that evening, the teacher adds a brief note to each pupil's own assessment, highlighting what they have achieved and commenting constructively on any difficulties they have identified.

FURTHER READING

A key text on assessment for learning in general is Black (2003). Another helpful book on the general issues in assessment for learning and teaching, written from a primary school perspective, is Briggs (2003). Hafeez provides a useful chapter, entitled 'Using assessment to improve teaching and learning' (in Thompson, 2003), which draws on the work of the Assessment Reform Group in relation to learning mathematics. For a thoughtful overview of the issues in assessment in mathematics and an analysis of the purposes of assessment in relation to the student, the teacher and the system, read the chapter by Niss on 'Assessment in mathematics education and its effects' (in Niss, 1993b).

RELATED ENTRIES

Assessment for teaching. Errors.

Assessment for teaching

DEFINITION

Assessment for teaching is when teachers make judgements about their pupils' knowledge, their ability to perform particular skills, their understanding of key concepts and principles, their attitudes and personal qualities, and so on, in order to help them in their job of teaching. Because assessment is such an integral part of the process of teaching, teachers assess their pupils frequently and in many different ways.

EXPLANATION AND DISCUSSION

As well as checking the written work of pupils, teachers assess their pupils, make judgements about their learning and monitor their progress at every stage of a lesson, in every interaction and observation that takes place in the classroom. They do this in a variety of ways, formal and informal, planned and unplanned. Some of the ways in which primary school teachers gather evidence about their pupils' learning in mathematics are by:

- noting how they respond to questions in class or contribute to class discussion;
- having one-to-one discussions with them about their work during the lesson;
- scrutinizing and marking their written work;
- asking pupils to make their own self-assessments of their learning;
- observing their contributions in practical and group activities;
- giving them occasional written or practical tests designed to assess particular objectives;
- analysing their results in formal, national or commercially produced tests.

Four important reasons related to the process of teaching for which primary school teachers assess their pupils are:

- to provide the teacher with information about the pupils' progress to inform their teaching and planning;
- to diagnose an individual pupil's problems;
- to group pupils for teaching purposes;
- to contribute to the teacher's evaluation of his or her teaching.

Assessment to inform teaching and planning

In terms of the process of teaching, the primary purpose of assessment is to discover the extent to which pupils are actually learning the material they are being taught, so that decisions can be made about current teaching approaches and plans for future lessons. The process starts by determining objectives for the pupils' learning. For example, for Year 3 pupils (7 to 8 years) an objective might be that they can use the fact that 'division is the inverse of multiplication and vice versa … to devise and record related multiplication and division number sentences' (DfES, 2006a: 41). The objective should be sufficiently clear and specific for the teacher to be able to plan in advance how they will determine whether or not it has been achieved. In this case, the teacher might expect the pupils for example, given 12 counters, to be able to arrange them in a rectangular array and then to write down two multiplications statements and two division statements that correspond to this array (such as $3 \times 4 = 12$, $4 \times 3 = 12$, $12 \div 4 = 3$ and $12 \div 3 = 4$). Having specified the objective and how it will be demonstrated, and then taught the mathematical material, it is relatively straightforward for the teacher to assess to what extent pupils have met the objective (see below). This information is then helpful for the teacher in deciding whether to revise or reinforce some particular mathematical skills for some pupils, whether to make adjustments to their plans, whether to find a different approach to teaching these skills, or whether they can confidently move on to new material that draws on these skills.

Assessment to diagnose individual problems

Sometimes teachers feel they need to work out why an individual pupil is having particular problems with some of the material they should be learning, to identify in detail the precise nature of the pupil's problems.

The distinctive nature of this diagnostic assessment is that it does not just determine that a pupil has failed to learn something, but attempts to determine the reasons why. Diagnostic assessment is especially important therefore with some pupils who have specific learning difficulties in mathematics. It is a time-consuming process, requiring in-depth, one-to-one conversations with the pupil and observation of their attempts to carry out mathematical procedures.

Assessment to group pupils for teaching purposes

Grouping pupils across classes into sets according to their ability is particularly common in mathematics where teachers find the difficulties of teaching the whole range of ability in one class to be especially challenging. Even where setting is not used it is common for pupils within a class to be put into groups for mathematics according to ability, so that different provision can be made at certain stages of the lesson. To undertake any such grouping or setting, teachers must assess their pupils. Such assessment should be done using a wide range of evidence, such as the teacher's own records of the pupils' progress against specific key objectives, the pupils' work over a period of time, the pupils' performances in various planned assessment tasks devised by the teacher, or the pupils' scores on some commercially produced or national tests.

Assessment to inform evaluation

The best teachers reflect continually on their teaching and systematically evaluate their own performance. Information obtained from the assessment of their pupils is one of the most significant components of the teacher's personal evaluation of their teaching. In making judgements about the effectiveness of their planning, their choices in teaching, their teaching methods, their classroom organization, their teaching style, their communication skills, and so on, teachers will be informed by the extent to which the evidence from their assessments indicates that these have resulted in the pupils learning what was intended.

PRACTICAL EXAMPLES

Here is an imaginary assessment note that might have been written by a teacher at the end of a lesson based on the example of the objective used above with a Year 3 class. It illustrates how different assessment methods can be used to gather evidence about pupils' learning and then this evidence used to inform teaching and planning.

The red group managed fine with the rectangular arrays and all of them seemed to be independently working out and writing down pairs of multiplication and division statements for arrays with 10, 12, 15 and 20 counters. They had a good discussion, initiated by Jack, about the fact that 12 and 20 could be done in more than one way. Jack then spotted that if you had 9 counters arranged in a square there would only be one multiplication and one division statement: a very creative bit of thinking. He was able to explain this to the rest of the class in the plenary session at the end of the lesson. This group would be ready now to find all the different ways you could arrange a number like 24 in arrays and write down all the corresponding multiplication and division results. The yellow and blue groups managed most of the examples, but there were a few random errors. I marked their written work later and they were scoring between 10 and 15 out of 24. I think I had better review this work in the oral/mental starter in tomorrow's lesson. The orange group had simpler numbers to work with, but three of them wrote their division statements the wrong way round (e.g. $2 \div 8 = 4$). I asked Jo what this number sentence said and she read it as '2 goes into 8 four times'. I'll make sure I deal with this error at the start of tomorrow's lesson and try to make the correct links with the language of division.

FURTHER READING

Clarke and Atkinson (1996) provide a practical and readable guide to assessment in mathematics in the primary school. The authors emphasize that the assessment process must enhance the child's learning and the teacher's teaching. Wright et al. (2005) show how the assessment tools of the Mathematics Recovery Programme, developed in Australia, can help teachers to diagnose the difficulties of those who underachieve in early numeracy. Headington (2000) gives useful guidance on assessment for trainee teachers, with illustrations of trainees' assessments of children's work.

RELATED ENTRIES

Assessment for learning. Differentiation. Errors. Questioning.

Cognitive Conflict

DEFINITION

Cognitive conflict is where learners are faced with discrepancies or conflicting ideas, or a result that differs from their prediction or conflicts with their existing understanding. The resolution of this conflict can lead to increased knowledge and understanding. Cognitive conflict in teaching mathematics can therefore be used to promote growth in understanding.

EXPLANATION AND DISCUSSION

Cognitive conflict is an important concept in the constructivist theory of learning. One of the main tenets of this theory is that learners construct their own knowledge through action and reflective thought. Learners bring their existing knowledge and beliefs with them to the learning environment and these prior experiences affect the development of conceptual understanding. Learners build understanding of a concept through an active process, using pre-existing knowledge, varied learning experiences and reflection. Pirie and Kieran (1992) describe this growth in understanding as 'a dynamic process of reorganization'. Understanding is not an all or nothing state, but depends on the richness of the connections of a concept with other pre-existing ideas. These cognitive structures have been referred to by Skemp (1971, latest edition 1993) as 'mental schemas', while Hiebert and Carpenter (1992) describe these 'as a web of related ideas'. According to Skemp, a schema integrates existing knowledge and acts as a tool for future learning, which implies that 'what we can learn with understanding depends on our currently available schemas' (1993: 139). When students encounter new information, they have to think about how the new knowledge fits with their existing knowledge.

In Piaget's (1977) terms, cognitive structures change through the process of adaptation, which involves assimilation and accommodation, in order to achieve equilibrium. Assimilation occurs when new knowledge fits with existing cognitive structures, and it is assimilated into the learner's schema. Accommodation occurs when learners rearrange their existing cognitive structures to make sense of new experiences and new knowledge. According to Piaget, equilibrium occurs in three stages. At first, learners are satisfied with their existing ideas and are in a state of equilibrium. Then they become aware of some of the limitations of their understanding and are now in a state of disequilibrium, and face cognitive conflict. If a better version of understanding can replace the old schema, through reconstruction (Skemp) or accommodation (Piaget), then equilibrium can be reached once more. Cognitive development consists of adapting to the environment by maintaining a balance of assimilation and accommodation.

These ideas are particularly relevant to children learning mathematics in primary school. In number work, for example, many concepts and principles are learnt first by children with reference only to positive whole numbers. Sometimes these can be extended to working with other kinds of numbers by a process of assimilation. For example, the concept of ordinal number (numbers on a number line) extends with little cognitive conflict to embrace negative numbers. But these new numbers can no longer be conceived of as representing sets of objects (the cardinal aspect of number). This is such a dominant component of the child's conception of what a number is that the new notion of a negative number causes cognitive conflict that has to be resolved by the process of accommodation. Many adults continue to find the concept of a negative number mysterious precisely because they have never been helped to achieve the restructuring required in their conception of what a number is.

One teaching strategy to promote cognitive development is deliberately to expose the learner to cognitive conflict. This approach involves providing opportunities where the learner's existing ideas are made explicit and then the learner is faced with a conflicting perspective. It is the resolution of these conflicting perspectives that leads to conceptual change. This use of cognitive conflict to promote cognitive development emphasizes the importance of considering the learner's existing ideas and conceptions. Cognitive conflict can also arise from discussion between learners sharing their methods of working out a problem. This peer discussion encourages learners to listen to another person's methods and ways of understanding and will often lead pupils with a naive or limited understanding of a mathematical idea to engage with cognitive conflict and modify their understanding to accommodate the ideas of other learners.

These approaches have been found to be particularly effective in teaching mathematics and science. In these subjects, concepts and principles are most clearly constructed on existing knowledge and understanding and it is therefore especially important that teachers take account of learners' limited or incorrect understandings, in devising their teaching approaches. Cognitive acceleration studies, which began with Cognitive Acceleration in Science Education (CASE) and later Cognitive Acceleration in Mathematics Education (CAME), demonstrated the effectiveness of using cognitive conflict to promote cognitive development in primary and secondary children (Adey and Shayer, 1990).

PRACTICAL EXAMPLES

Below are three examples of where cognitive conflict may be used by a teacher to challenge a pupil's initial response to mathematical situations and ideas.

Set diagrams

When children sort numbers into sets, they are provided initially with two separate circles, as shown in Figure 2. Learners might, for example, be asked to sort the following numbers into two groups, multiples of 3 and even numbers: 2, 3, 4, 8, 9, 10, 15, 20, 21. If numbers such as 6, 12 and 18 are introduced, learners are faced with the situation that these numbers belong in both sets, since they are multiples of 3 *and* even. This cognitive conflict, with the teacher helping the learners to articulate the difficulty that needs to be resolved, can lead to the learners working out for themselves that the sets need to overlap to allow for numbers in both sets. In this way they have been helped by the resolution of the cognitive conflict to a better understanding of the ways in which sets of numbers can relate to each other.

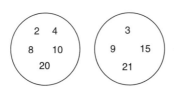

Figure 2 *Cognitive conflict in sorting numbers into two sets*

Figure 3 *Children's visualization of water in a tilted tumbler*

Visualization

This is one of the activities used in the CAME study (Adey et al., 2002). Learners are shown a transparent tumbler with water inside. They are then asked to imagine the tumbler being tilted to one side and to draw it with the water inside. Many children draw the water level parallel to the top of the tumbler rather than parallel to the ground, as illustrated in Figure 3. To provide the cognitive conflict for learners to reorganize their ideas, a horizontal line could be drawn on the actual tumbler, to show the level of the water; the tumbler would then be tipped slowly and the children asked what they notice and to compare this with their predictions.

ADDING FRACTIONS

Learners often apply inappropriately the procedures they have learnt with whole numbers to new calculations with fractions. For example, when asked to calculate $\frac{1}{2} + \frac{1}{4}$ pupils may misapply their existing addition schema to produce answers such as $\frac{1}{6}$ or $\frac{2}{6}$. Presenting the problem in a diagram, such as Figure 4, can provide the cognitive

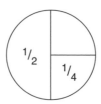

Figure 4 *Showing that 1/2 added to 1/4 does not give 1/6 or 2/6*

conflict necessary for a learner to realize that what works for addition of whole numbers does not work for adding fractions. This realization is an important experience for many pupils in moving towards some understanding of how to calculate with fractions.

FURTHER READING

The significance of cognitive conflict in mathematics teaching is illustrated in chapter 2 of Haylock and Cockburn (2003). Their account of the mathematical development of the concept of number shows how learners' new experiences of number require adaptation of existing understandings as they contend with unstable truths, changing properties and new possibilities. Hiebert et al. (1997) present a framework of five dimensions for promoting understanding in teaching mathematics. In the third of these – the social culture of the classroom – the authors discuss the idea of creating cognitive conflict as an effective way of deepening pupils' understanding. Skemp (1993) proposes a theory of understanding in mathematics being developed through reconstruction of existing schemas that is particularly relevant to the notion of cognitive conflict.

RELATED ENTRIES

Constructivism. Concept learning. Errors.

Concept Learning

DEFINITION

Concept learning is a process by which a learner organizes their experiences, abstracting from a number of exemplars what it is that they have in common and using one concept name to embrace them all. The concept can be said to be learnt when the pupil has formulated an abstraction that exists in its own right without having to be attached to any particular concrete examples.

EXPLANATION AND DISCUSSION

Every field of human learning is characterized by its key concepts. In primary mathematics, the numerous concepts to be learnt would include, for example, 'three', 'triangle', 'square', 'multiple', 'factor', 'prime number', 'reflective symmetry', 'angle', 'right angle', 'difference'. Learning concepts usually involves: shaping the concept through encountering exemplars and non-exemplars; associating the concept with its name; abstraction; articulation of the critical attributes of the exemplars of the concept; formulation of a definition; applying the definition to difficult cases; refinement of the definition. It should not be assumed, however, that all concept learning moves systematically through these stages. Learning is always messier and less systematic than might be implied by the structured models of educational psychology.

Each concept to be learnt is an abstraction from a number of exemplars of the concept. For example, in learning the concept of 'square' pupils meet many shapes to which the word 'square' is attached. They begin to recognize intuitively the shared attributes of these shapes, although they may not actually articulate what these are in the early stages of concept formation. They learn to ignore the ways in which the shapes called squares are different (such as their size or their orientation). To help the formation of the concept, pupils need also to encounter non-exemplars, shapes that are *not* associated with the word 'square', as illustrated in Figure 5.

Gradually, the abstract concept of 'square' is developed, so that pupils can bring to mind the abstraction, 'a square', as something that exists in their mind independently of any particular concrete examples.

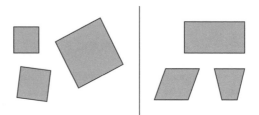

Figure 5 *Exemplars and non-exemplars of the concept of 'square'*

The teacher will use questioning to draw the pupil's attention to the significant shared attributes of all those shapes that are called squares and how these are not present in the non-exemplars of the concept. A significant point to note, however, is that usually the learning of concepts does not start with the presentation of a definition or a statement of the key attributes. Good teaching will not start by saying: 'Today we are going to learn about squares. A square is a four-sided shape in which all the sides are equal in length and all the angles are right angles.' Usually the definition comes after the concept has been developed intuitively through informal discussion and classification of exemplars and non-exemplars. A 5-year-old, for example, can have a well-formed concept of 'square' without any notion of what is a right angle and without the skills required to check the equality of the lengths of the sides. But the definition is required at some stage, particularly to check difficult cases. For example, older pupils who have also learnt the concept of 'rectangle' will require the definition of a rectangle to decide whether or not a square is also a rectangle.

This illustrates a common difficulty for pupils in concept learning, where one concept is a subset of another or where two concepts overlap. A younger pupil may have difficulty in recognizing the shape in Figure 6 as a square, preferring to classify it as a 'diamond shape' (technically, a rhombus). This may be because the attributes they associate intuitively with 'diamond shape' impact on their mind more strongly than those of a square when the shape is presented in this orientation. Rotating the paper may convince the child that it is actually a square, but it is quite likely that a younger pupil will think that it turns into a square when you rotate it and it turns back into a diamond when you rotate it back again! Only the later application of the definition of a square will completely resolve this kind of difficulty. But clearly this will have to wait until the pupil has developed the concepts and skills involved in the definition, which paradoxically can sometimes be more difficult to grasp than the concept which is being defined.

Sometimes the consideration of difficult or ambiguous cases will lead to a refinement of the definition. For example, the concept of rotational

Figure 6   *Is this shape a square?*

symmetry might emerge from consideration of exemplars as the property that a two-dimensional shape has when it can be rotated to fit exactly onto an image of itself. However, there is an ambiguity to be addressed here, namely, what happens when any two-dimensional shape is rotated through 360°. This consideration would lead to a refinement of the first attempt at a definition of the concept.

Skemp (1993) distinguishes between primary concepts, which are learnt directly from sensory and motor experiences, and higher order concepts, which are concepts abstracted from other concepts. So, for example, 'three' might be considered a primary concept, abstracted from many simple examples of sets of three things. But 'prime number' would be a much higher-order concept, of which 'three' is an exemplar. The greater the extent to which an abstraction is distanced from concrete experience, the higher the order of the concept being learnt. Skemp makes the point that the challenges of learning mathematics are that it involves mainly higher-order concepts that are so much more abstract than those we encounter in everyday life and that the direction of learning is always towards greater abstraction. The implication is that secure learning of lower-order concepts is essential for later learning of those that are more abstract and of a higher order.

One other difficulty associated with conceptual development in mathematics is that some key concepts that pupils learn in their early years are of necessity incomplete, naive or in some way watered down. For example, pupils might develop a concept of 'number' as the number of objects in a set, which may be adequate and appropriate for their early experiences of counting. However, if they are later to embrace within the concept of 'number' such experiences as ordinal numbers, number lines, fractional numbers, decimals, negative numbers, numbers used for measuring, and so on, then the concept will have to change, enlarge and develop. This process may involve considerable cognitive conflict, which will either be resolved by the learners accommodating their new experiences and rearranging their earlier understanding of the concept, or will lead them to abandon their attempts to make any sense of mathematics.

PRACTICAL EXAMPLES

There is space here for just one further illustration of how mathematical concepts are developed and form the basis for higher-order concepts.

Pupils will encounter many examples of one number being divided exactly by another, such as 28 being divided exactly by 4, 12 being divided exactly by 3, and so on. In other cases pupils will find that the division does not work out exactly, such as when 19 is divided by 4, or 11 is divided by 3. These observations are already building on abstract concepts, such as whole numbers, division and remainders. Provided these concepts are secure, there is then the possibility that the teacher may lead the pupils to abstract from these exemplars and non-exemplars the higher-order concept of 'factor': 4 is a factor of 28, 3 is a factor of 12, 4 is not a factor of 19, and 3 is not a factor of 11.

Because the concept of a factor is clearly a higher-order abstraction, teachers will seek to bring it within the grasp of pupils in primary schools by embedding it as far as possible in concrete or pictorial representations (see, for example, Haylock, 2006: 123). Pupils can be led then to formulate a definition of a factor, as a number that divides exactly into another number, and to apply this to other examples. They can then use the definition to consider difficult cases. For example, is 7 a factor of 7? Is 1 a factor of anything? Is 0 a factor of anything? Is 3.5 a factor of 7? Addressing these questions may well lead to refinement of the definition.

Once the concept is securely understood it can then be built on to develop other higher-order concepts, such as 'prime number'. Again, this begins by observing and discussing exemplars and non-exemplars. In investigating factors we see that some numbers, such as 2, 3, 5, 7 and 11, have only two factors, 1 and themselves. These are the exemplars of the new concept, prime numbers. Others, such as 4, 6, 8, 9 and 10, are seen to have more than two factors. These are the non-exemplars, non-primes. A definition is formulated (such as, a prime number has only two factors, 1 and itself) and applied to other examples. Then the difficult case can be considered: is 1 a prime number? This again leads to a refinement of the definition: a prime number is one that has exactly two factors (so 1 is not prime). (See Haylock, 2006: 124–5.)

FURTHER READING

A thorough discussion of concept learning in general is provided in chapter 7 of Child (2007), now in its 8th edition. Chapter 2 of Liebeck

(1984) is a very accessible account of concept formation in the early years of learning mathematics.

RELATED ENTRIES

Cognitive conflict. Equivalence. Principle learning.

Conservation of Quantity

DEFINITION

In mathematics and science, conservation of quantity refers to the principle that quantities such as number, length, mass and volume are invariant under certain transformations. Pupils' confident and appropriate use of the principle of conservation of such quantities is a key indicator of their developing understanding.

EXPLANATION AND DISCUSSION

Conservation of mass is the principle that the mass of a certain quantity of material is unchanged if the material is transformed in shape or position. A lump of dough still has the same mass when it is rolled out into a sausage shape or broken up into a number of smaller balls or even taken to the moon. Conservation of volume is the principle involved in recognizing that the volume of water in a beaker is not changed by pouring the water into a differently shaped beaker, even though the height of the water in the second beaker may be greater or less than that in the first (see Figure 7).

The principle of conservation of quantity – along with transitivity – was identified by the influential educational psychologist, Jean Piaget, as one of the key indicators of the development of children's understanding. Testing individual children on various tasks related to conservation,

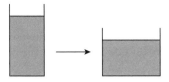

Figure 7   *The principle of conservation of volume*

he concluded that most children grasped the principle of conservation of number around the age of 5 to 6 years. In a typical Piagetian task for assessing understanding of conservation of number he would show the child six bottles and six glasses and ask them questions about whether the numbers of glasses and bottles were still the same after one or the other had been rearranged, spread out or grouped together more closely (Piaget, 1952). Piaget claimed that the ideas of conservation of length and area developed around the ages of 6 to 7 years, followed by conservation of mass and weight, with conservation of volume not fully grasped by most children until the age of 11 to 12 years (Piaget and Inhelder, 1972).

Piaget's rigid ideas about the development of understanding of conservation have been challenged by many other researchers, with criticism of the abstract, clinical context in which his work was done and the style of his questioning. Donaldson (1986) demonstrated that children as young as 4 years would show a grasp of the principle of conservation of number when the questions posed to them were embedded in meaningful contexts, for example, when playing games with teddy bears.

A major criticism of Piaget's work is his failure to take into account the child's response to the social aspects of the test situation. McGarrigle and Donaldson (1974) showed how children's responses to conservation tasks are influenced by their perception of what it is the adult asking the questions wants. So, a child who is asked more than once if the number of bottles is different from the number of glasses may well change their answer in order to respond in a way that they think will please the adult. So Piaget's findings are often not consistent with the observations of primary school teachers in the social context of the classroom. For example, pupils much younger than 11 years – in a situation where they are really thirsty – will not be fooled into choosing a smaller drink of juice if the teacher pours the juice into a narrower beaker.

A significant question for the primary school teacher is whether understanding of conservation arises naturally through maturation or can be developed through focused teaching. This question is not addressed by Piaget's work and not resolved by the research that has followed in this area.

PRACTICAL EXAMPLES

Primary school teachers will recognize the principle of conservation of number as a significant component of children's understanding of counting and operations with number, and will plan specific activities that incorporate this principle. For example, the teacher may hide a subset of counters from a set of 10 and ask the children to count the remaining counters and, then by counting on determine how many counters are hidden. Simple interactive tasks such as this clearly assume that the child grasps the fact that there are still 10 counters even when they cannot see them all: in other words, the number is conserved. In running a task like this, inevitably the teacher will ask children how many counters there are altogether, both before the subset is hidden and after. Similarly, any kind of activity involving measuring liquid volume by pouring water into various measuring containers must assume that the volume is unchanged in the process.

Most primary teachers, when appropriate, include practical activities and discussion with children that challenge children's naive ideas and provide opportunities to make the principles of conservation of number and conservation in various measuring concepts explicit. For example, some 8-year-olds might be given two balls of play-dough and asked to use some weighing scales to determine which is heavier. Each child in turn is then challenged to re-mould or rearrange the lighter ball of dough in some way to try to make it heavier than the other. The discussion that ensues will eventually lead to children saying things like, 'You can't make it heavier, whatever you do to it!' In this way, through the challenge of a game, the principle of conservation of weight is articulated by the children in a context that makes sense to them.

Generally, such activities and discussions, embedded in realistic contexts and done with an awareness about the ways in which children engage with questioning in the classroom, will prove to be effective learning experience at ages younger than those predicted by Piaget's findings about children's understanding of conservation.

FURTHER READING

In her classic book, *Children's Minds* (first published in 1978, republished in 1986), Margaret Donaldson provides a research-based critique of

Piaget's work on the development of children's understanding. Teachers of young children find that Donaldson's work resonates strongly with their own experience. Chapter 6 of Haylock and Cockburn (2003) discusses the mathematics of conservation in measurement contexts and provides an example of a small-group game that can promote discussion of the principle. Chapter 12, 'Cognition: Piaget's theory', in Smith et al. (2003), provides a thorough account of Piaget's theory of children's development, including the significance of conservation in this.

RELATED ENTRIES

Equivalence. Meaningful context. Transformation. Transitivity.

Constructivism

DEFINITION

The central idea of constructivism is that learning is an active process in which learners construct new ideas or concepts based upon their current and prior knowledge. Knowledge is not waiting 'out there' to be acquired, but is constructed. Different writers place more or less emphasis on the individual or on the social aspects of how knowledge is constructed. Constructivism is a theory about learning and therefore has relevance to what constitutes an effective mathematical classroom environment.

EXPLANATION AND DISCUSSION

Few teachers would argue against the idea that learners need to construct knowledge. Behaviourist theories of transmitting knowledge to learners are now out of fashion as it has become clear that when we teach or tell learners something, we cannot assume they will make sense of it in the way we intend. It seems that each learner internalizes the knowledge and makes sense of it in an individual way. Teachers see this in the classroom when they think they have taught or covered something, only to find that pupils make mistakes or ask questions that reveal they have not understood the knowledge as they intended.

Although constructivism is about the individual making sense of the world, it is not synonymous with discovery learning, because the role of the teacher is of central importance. Clearly, to be most effective, teachers need to understand how pupils learn. Constructivism focuses attention on the pupil's learning rather than on the teacher's teaching. We can talk about a constructivist view of learning, but not constructivist teaching as this is a contradiction. Rather than thinking up perfect definitions or explanations of concepts and skills, the challenge for teachers is to create experiences that engage pupils and foster the making of mathematical meaning, which can be applied or transferred to other situations.

Constructivism as a theory of learning is more than simply 'learning by doing' or experiential learning. Although practical activities may go some way towards helping children to build up knowledge, practical apparatus is not sufficient as in itself it does not embody a concept. Children may manipulate mathematical materials in the prescribed way but may not be learning, or they might not be able to transfer their knowledge to more formal representations or to other contexts. What is also needed is reflection on the activity. This might be individual reflection but will more often be promoted through discussion with the teacher or with peers.

Discussions about constructivism usually include the definition of radical constructivism by von Glaserfeld (1995: 18), which makes these two claims:

- knowledge is not passively received but actively built up by the cognizing subject;
- the function of cognition is adaptive and serves the organization of the experiential world, not the discovery of ontological reality.

This constructivist model is based on Piaget's ideas of the individual organizing their world through the processes of assimilation, accommodation and equilibration to fit their experiences. Other writers (Ernest, 1991; Harries and Spooner, 2000; Merttens, 1996) argue that we need to take more account of the social influences of learning, and the role of discussion and negotiation. This has led to the idea of social constructivism. This is a branch of constructivism owing its origins to Bruner, who stressed the importance of the teacher, and to Vygotsky. The major theme of Vygotsky's theoretical framework is that social interaction plays a fundamental role in the development of cognition. Vygotsky (1978: 57) states: 'Every function in the child's cultural development appears twice: first, on the social level, and later, on the individual level; first, between people (interpsychological) and then inside the child (intrapsychological).' A second aspect of Vygotsky's theory is the idea that the potential for cognitive development depends upon the 'zone of proximal development'. This idea is that through scaffolding by adult guidance or peer collaboration children can extend their knowledge, skills or understanding beyond what can be attained alone.

As Harries and Spooner (2000: 28) argue, 'knowledge is ... socially constructed between groups who share meanings and social perspectives of a common world'. Much has been written on the value of discussion in the mathematics classroom as an important way in which pupils learn mathematics. Social constructivism goes beyond this, as Orton (2004: 198) explains: 'the claims of socio-constructivism are that meaning or understanding is being actively *negotiated* through such discussion' (original emphasis). This leads to the idea of pupils building up shared understanding as a group, or even as a whole class.

In practical terms, then, what does this mean for the mathematics classroom? If the implication of constructivism is that there is more to teaching than just telling or trying to transmit knowledge to pupils, how can teachers foster the development of mathematical knowledge? Carpenter and Lehrer (1999: 19–32), adopting a constructivist model, identified five forms of mental activity that promote mathematical understanding. The teacher's role is to ensure that pupils engage in these kinds of mental activity:

1. constructing relationships;
2. extending and applying mathematical knowledge;
3. reflecting about the experience;
4. articulating what one knows;
5. making mathematical knowledge one's own.

PRACTICAL EXAMPLES

An example of an activity for older pupils in the primary school illustrates how these five features of the constructivist model might apply.

Children often have difficulty interpreting distance–time graphs (typically graphs of journeys) and often mistake the graph for a picture of the actual movement, rather than a relationship between two variables (distance and time). Grant (1996) describes how these misinterpretations may be overcome if a dynamic, kinaesthetic environment is created through the use of a data logger (distance sensor) to record the distance of an object at different times in order to generate distance–time graphs. When pupils move in front of the distance sensor, they create their own distance–time graphs.

Constructing relationships

The teacher asks the pupil to interpret what happens in the graph when they make various movements in front of the sensor. Pupils are able to make connections between the direction and speed of their movements with the shape of the graph that is generated. In this way they are engaged in constructing relationships.

Extending and applying mathematical knowledge

Pupils extend their learning from interpreting the relationship between their movements and the graph to applying the relationship to generate a particular shape of graph. The teacher encourages pupils to set themselves various challenges, such as, 'Can I make the graph symmetrical?' and poses other questions, such as 'Can you make a circle?' or 'Which capital letters can be made?'

Reflecting about the experience

Other pupils make suggestions and a rich discussion ensues. Ideas are tried out and refined. Pupils are asked why various things happen. The movement and graphs are reflected upon, discussed and meaning is constructed.

Articulating what one knows

The teacher gives pupils opportunities to summarize what has been learnt so far, and, using questioning about the steepness of various parts of the graphs generated, encourages pupils to articulate precisely what it is about a movement that affects the gradient of a graph.

Making mathematical knowledge one's own

Each pupil in the group has been actively engaged in constructing their own meaning from their own engagement with the activity, their personal reflection, their contribution to discussion and the articulation of their own experience. Because of this and because the mathematics is not simply material that has been transmitted to them by the teacher, the pupils have a sense of ownership of what they have learnt.

FURTHER READING

Chapter 2 of Harries and Spooner (2000) gives a clear overview of various learning theories, including a helpful summary of constructivism. Theory into Practice (http://tip.psychology.org) is a useful website that outlines some of the major theories of learning and instruction. Constructivism is not without its critics; anyone seriously interested in how the mind works should read Pinker (1998), particularly his section on mathematics and his critique of some of the less well-considered assertions of constructivists (pp. 338–42).

RELATED ENTRIES

Cognitive conflict. Investigation (enquiry). Making connections. Talk.

Creativity in Mathematics

DEFINITION

The notion of creativity is used in education in many different ways. A helpful definition is provided by the National Advisory Committee on Creative and Cultural Education (NACCCE, 1999: 30): creativity is 'imaginative activity fashioned so as to produce outcomes that are both original and of value'. This definition incorporates four principles: that creativity must involve thinking or behaving imaginatively; that this must be for some purpose; that the product must be in some sense original; but that it must also be of some value or appropriate to the objective of the task. In these terms, the notion of creativity has relevance to children in primary schools responding to mathematical challenges and solving mathematical problems.

EXPLANATION AND DISCUSSION

Creativity in mathematics is a higher category of ability that is distinct from attainment in conventional tests of mathematical skills, knowledge and understanding. Responding to concerns that the National Curriculum in England and its associated national tests had resulted in a narrowing of children's experience in primary schools, the government launched a policy document for primary schools in 2003, designed to foster enjoyment as well as excellence (DfES, 2003: 4). 'Creativity' is one of the key words in this document. However, the word is used loosely and is inevitably associated with what are perceived as 'creative subjects'. For example, the document says that 'as well as giving them the essential tools for learning, primary education is about children experiencing the joy of discovery, solving problems, being creative in writing, art, music ...'. There is clearly potential here for mathematics being categorized as one of the 'essential tools' and any notion of mathematical creativity being limited to vaguely artistic activities in mathematics lessons, such as constructing shapes and geometric patterns. A more significant construct for mathematical creativity in school children will incorporate the four strands of the NACCCE definition of creativity given above.

Imaginative activity

First, in relation to imaginative activity, creativity in primary school mathematics should be discussed in terms of the cognitive processes that are particularly significant in terms of children doing mathematics. These include thinking divergently and flexibly (being open to many possibilities), rather than just thinking convergently (always looking for just one acceptable response), the breaking of mental sets and overcoming of fixations in solving mathematical problems. An intriguing question in mathematical problem solving is this: Why is it that I cannot solve a mathematical problem when I have available all the mathematical skills and knowledge required? Often, the answer is that I am limiting my thinking because of some mental set or fixation. A characteristic of creative problem solving in mathematics is the willingness to be open to considering a number of different approaches, to overcome a fixation on the first approach that comes to mind, or to break from a mental set which might be suggested by the style or content of the problem. The enemies of creative thinking in mathematics are rigidity in processing mathematical information and an adherence in all circumstances to routine procedures and stereotype approaches.

Purposefulness

Within any given field, creativity, to have any validity, must be for some purpose. In mathematics, children in primary schools will have opportunities for this kind of creative thinking when they are responding to non-routine mathematical questions or challenges, seeking non-standard but more elegant ways of carrying out mathematical processes, looking at a situation and posing interesting mathematical problems, carrying out mathematical investigations, solving mathematical problems or applying their mathematical skills and knowledge to the solution of problems in other mathematical areas.

Originality

As well as displaying qualities such as flexibility and openness, creative responses to mathematical questions and challenges or solutions to mathematical problems will be recognized as being, in some sense, original. In the context of a primary classroom, it is unlikely that responses of pupils will be original in universal terms, and it is often difficult to identify what counts as original thinking for an individual child. The criterion of originality is therefore best understood as meaning 'original compared with the peer group'. Teachers can recognize as original an unusual response that is produced by only one or two pupils in a class.

Appropriateness

Such original responses must also be appropriate and of value in terms of mathematical criteria and the objectives of the task in hand. For example, 67 might be an original response to 'What is 7 multiplied by 8?' but it is mathematically incorrect, and therefore of no value. An original approach to solving a problem is not creative if it is actually of no value at all in terms of obtaining a solution and if it ignores the constraints of the situation being considered.

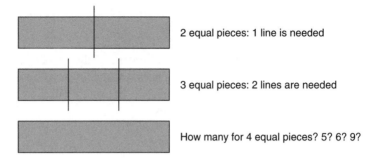

Figure 8 *Overcoming a mental set*

PRACTICAL EXAMPLES

Some examples of the ways in which teachers might promote and recognize creative thinking in mathematics are given below.

Overcoming a mental set

In Figure 8, pupils are shown that 1 line is needed to cut the rectangle into 2 equal pieces and 2 lines to cut it into 3 equal pieces. They are asked how many lines are needed to cut it into 4 equal pieces, 5 equal pieces, 6 equal pieces and 9 equal pieces. The 'non-creative' responses are 3, 4, 5 and 8, respectively. A pupil can show mathematical creativity by overcoming the mental set established in the first two cases to come up with solutions using 2 lines for 4 pieces, 3 lines for 6 pieces and 4 lines for 9 pieces.

Divergent thinking

Pupils can be given opportunities to show flexibility and originality by mathematical tasks modelled on the classic divergent thinking tests developed in the early years of creativity research by American researchers such as Torrance (1966). For example, pupils might be given $27 \times 92 = 2484$ and asked to deduce as many other number facts from this result as they can. A mathematically creative pupil would consider, for example, the possibilities of generating new results by using operations other than multiplication (such as $2484 \div 27 = 92$) and numbers other than whole numbers (such as $13.5 \times 92 = 1242$).

Posing mathematical questions

Pupils can show flexibility and originality by making up mathematical questions that could be answered about a given situation. For example, some younger pupils might be given a collection of containers and a supply of water and invited to make up as many different questions as they can about the containers, which they could answer. A group of older primary pupils might be given a copy of a daily newspaper and challenged to pose interesting mathematical questions about the newspaper that they might investigate.

Non-routine problems

Teachers can give pupils non-routine mathematical problems which require only very basic mathematical skills, but which require a creative, non-standard use of these skills in order to find a solution. The following two problems (adapted from Krutetskii, 1976: 149, 131), for example, require only very simple arithmetic, but some creative thinking about the numbers involved.

1. Two pupils want to buy a chocolate bar. They each have some money, but one is 25p short and the other 2p short. So they decide to pool their money. But they still don't have enough to buy the chocolate bar. How much is it?
2. A teacher gave a number to a pupil and asked her to subtract 3 from it and divide by 2. The pupil was not paying attention and instead she added 2 to the number and divided by 3. But she was lucky and still got the right answer! What was the given number?

FURTHER READING

Those who teach in the early years are referred to Kaltman (2005). In an enjoyable and stimulating book, Kaltman provides strategies for a play-based curriculum that reflect the importance of promoting creativity in young children in all areas of the curriculum, including mathematics. Some examples of how creative thinking in primary school mathematics can be recognized and encouraged can be found in the chapter on mathematical reasoning in Haylock (2006: 318–20). The QCA materials, 'Creativity: Find it, Promote it' (QCA website, www.ncaction.org.uk), provide information and case study examples designed to encourage teachers to promote pupils' creativity. At the time of writing the mathematical examples are limited, but there are some helpful principles about recognizing and promoting creativity in general that can be applied to mathematics in primary schools.

RELATED ENTRIES

Gender and mathematics. Giftedness in mathematics. Investigation (enquiry). Problem solving.

Cross-Cultural Mathematics

DEFINITION

The development of mathematical ideas has a long and rich history, to which many cultures have contributed. All peoples, the world over, engage in mathematics, albeit with varying number systems and methods of calculating. Cross-cultural mathematics is mathematical experience that draws on and makes explicit the contributions of different cultures. Incorporating cross-cultural ideas and activities in their mathematical experience can help primary pupils to broaden their understanding of how mathematical knowledge has developed and their appreciation of the contributions of many cultures to the current body of knowledge.

EXPLANATION AND DISCUSSION

Mathematics is universal in that 'people all over the world and in all eras of history have engaged in mathematics activities to the extent of their needs and interests' (Zaslavsky, 1996: 205). Mathematics is sometimes thought of as a non-cultural, value-free subject. Indeed, this apparent objectivity is what appeals to some learners. That this is a mistaken view is evidenced, for example, by the way in which the school mathematics curriculum in Britain has been shaped in recent years by political, social and economic demands (Askew, 2001; Brown, 2001; Reynolds and Muijs, 1999). Throughout history, the development of mathematics has been driven by economic, technological and scientific needs: from the advances in geometry achieved by the ancient Greeks with their requirements for land measurement and their architectural aspirations; through the invention of calculus in England and Germany in the seventeenth century in the context of the rapidly expanding field of scientific research; to the changing nature of mathematics in today's world of information technology. Pupils should appreciate therefore that mathematics is not a static body of knowledge, sitting out there in its final, complete state, just waiting to be transmitted into their minds. In all cultures, at all times, it has been developing and continues to develop, in ways that reflect the prevailing cultural values and expectations.

Exploring multicultural aspects of mathematics can enhance pupils' understanding of how and why mathematical ideas have developed. Cross-cultural examples can be used to present a more accurate picture of the history of mathematics, raising awareness of the contributions of different cultures to what pupils might wrongly regard as a Western European invention. For example, although the theorem of Pythagoras is named after a Greek mathematician, there is evidence of this theorem being used by the Chinese at least a thousand years earlier and even earlier by the Babylonians (Swetz and Kao, 1977).

Cross-cultural mathematical experiences can help children to appreciate that all peoples do mathematics, and such activities can therefore make mathematics appear more inclusive and inviting for pupils of all kinds of backgrounds. Referring to peoples of different nationalities and cultures, Zaslavsky points out: 'They all count objects, they measure various quantities, they invent calendars and other ways to describe the passage of time, they design works of art, they plan buildings, and they play games that involve mathematical concepts. Furthermore, they invent terminology that enables them to discuss these activities' (1996: 1).

By choosing appropriate examples, teachers can help children to appreciate these similarities, avoiding the possibility of the mathematics of other cultures being perceived as less developed, less significant or less sophisticated.

PRACTICAL EXAMPLES

Three examples of cross-cultural mathematical experiences are provided below.

The history of zero

Many children encounter difficulties with using zero in calculations, both as a number in its own right and as a placeholder in a multidigit number. It may be encouraging and instructive for pupils to discover, therefore, that zero was a challenging concept for many civilizations in the history of numeration systems. Teachers in primary schools can explore this history with their pupils. They can discover, for example, how the ancient Babylonians developed a place value system of numeration, but were hindered by the lack of a symbol for zero. They can learn about the Mayas, who lived in central America, occupying the area which is now southern Mexico, Guatemala, and northern Belize, who by AD 665 were using a base-twenty place value system, with a symbol for zero (Zaslavsky, 1996). Pupils can find out that the numeration system that we use today has its roots in a base-ten place value system developed in India, how a symbol for zero to occupy an empty place in a multidigit number was introduced, and how only later (by AD 650) did the concept of zero as a number in its own right emerge, again in Indian mathematics, first as a word and later as a symbol. The history is fascinating and draws on many cultures. Indian ideas spread east to China as well as west to the Islamic countries, via Arab traders, and came much later into Europe. In *Liber Abaci*, the Italian mathematician, Fibonacci, described the nine Indian symbols together with the sign 0 in around 1200. But the system was not widely adopted for a long time after that, because of the reluctance of Italian merchants to move away from Roman numerals. Eventually, in the fifteenth century, with the growth of trade and the availability of paper, the Hindu-Arabic numerals and the base-10 place value system that we use today became more widely established, as people recognized the advantages of the new system for calculations. (Source: 'MacTutor History of Mathematics' website, www.groups.dcs.st-and.ac.uk)

Vedic square

The Vedas represent some of the earliest Indian mathematical texts, dating from around 1000 BC (Nelson et al., 1993). The Vedic square shown

X	1	2	3	4	5	6	7	8	9
1	1	2	3	4	5	6	7	8	9
2	2	4	6	8	1	3	5	7	9
3	3	6	9	3	6	9	3	6	9
4	4	8	3	7	2	6	1	5	9
5	5	1	6	2	7	3	8	4	9
6	6	3	9	6	3	9	6	3	9
7	7	5	3	1	8	6	4	2	9
8	8	7	6	5	4	3	2	1	9
9	9	9	9	9	9	9	9	9	9

Figure 9 *A Vedic square*

in Figure 9 is an adaptation of the 1–9 multiplication table. The entries in the cells of this table are the digital roots of the products (see Haylock, 2006: 121–2): any product with more than one digit is replaced by a single digit number, obtained by successively summing the separate digits (for example, from $7 \times 8 = 56$, to $5 + 6 = 11$, then $1 + 1 = 2$). Once the grid is completed, there are many interesting patterns to discover. As well as looking for number patterns, the 'shape' of each number can be found. For example, if all the 1s are joined with straight lines a hexagon is formed – which can be used to make a tessellation (see Haylock, 2006: 286–9). Similarly, the 'shape' of the other numerals from 2 to 9 can be explored. This activity makes a pleasing link between number and the geometric patterns of Islamic art.

The Egyptians

This is a popular history topic in schools providing a number of opportunities for mathematical activities. For example, the Egyptian pyramids are a familiar and interesting shape for most pupils in primary schools. Pupils can easily draw the net of a square-based pyramid on card, adding some flaps for gluing the model together after cutting it out and folding it, to form the three-dimensional shape. This can be the starting point for designing the nets for other pyramids (triangle based, pentagon based, and so on). Pupils will also benefit from learning about the Egyptian numeration system, which had hieroglyphic symbols for one, ten, a hundred, a thousand, ten thousand, a hundred thousand, and a million, but no symbol for zero. Although based on powers of 10, this was not a place value system. Pupils can be invited to attempt various calculations using the Egyptian system for numbers; in so doing they will gain insights into the benefits and power of the principle of place value that underpins the system of numeration that we use today. The Egyptian use of fractions is a further intriguing piece of mathematics. These were mainly written using sums of unit fractions (where the numerator is one). For example $^2/_5$ would be written as $^1/_3 + ^1/_{15}$ and $^7/_8$ would be written as $^1/_2 + ^1/_4 + ^1/_8$.

FURTHER READING

Zaslavsky (1996), quoted above, is both informative and full of practical classroom ideas. The 'MacTutor History of Mathematics' website (www-groups.dcs.st-and.ac.uk) is a mine of information. Cross-cultural mathematics as described in this entry clearly make a significant contribution to achieving the aims of education within a multicultural society. For consideration of what this might mean in general in primary schools, see the chapter by Thangata on this subject (in Browne and Haylock, 2004).

RELATED ENTRIES

Cross-curricular mathematics. Home as a context for numeracy.

Cross-Curricular Mathematics

DEFINITION

Cross-curricular mathematics can be understood in three ways. First, other areas of the primary school curriculum can be seen as providing opportunities to use and apply the skills and knowledge that pupils learn in mathematics lessons in purposeful activities. Second, other curriculum areas can be seen as providing meaningful contexts within which mathematical concepts can be introduced or developed. Third, mathematics can be seen as one of a number of curriculum areas that might come together in an extended cross-curricular project of some kind, which is not located in any particular subject area in the school timetable.

EXPLANATION AND DISCUSSION

The structure of the National Curriculum in England (DfEE, 1999a), in which mathematics is presented as one of a number of discrete subjects with its own programme of study, attainment targets and national tests, may suggest that mathematics and the other curriculum subjects are to be taught separately, within their own slots in the school timetable. The National Numeracy Strategy (DfEE, 1999b), with its insistence on a daily mathematics lesson (the 'numeracy hour') and its framework of objectives, yearly programmes and examples of pupils' achievements in mathematics, appeared to reinforce this perception. As a consequence, in the first few years of the current millennium an observer visiting primary schools in England may have been hard pressed to find any examples of teachers embracing cross-curricular approaches to mathematics.

This is not to say that the potential of cross-curricular mathematics was not recognized in these policy documents. The National Curriculum programme of study for Key Stage 2 (7 to 11 years) states that pupils should be taught the knowledge, skills and understanding in a number of ways, including 'using mathematics in their work in other subjects' (DfEE, 1999a: 74). However, there is no parallel statement for Key Stage 1 (5 to 7 years), where it might be expected that rigid divisions between subjects would be less appropriate. The Numeracy Strategy states that better numeracy standards occur when teachers make links 'between mathematics and other subjects' (DfEE, 1999b: 5). The framework contains the following advice to teachers.

Mathematics contributes to many subjects of the primary curriculum, often in practical ways. Activities such as recording the growth of a plant, measuring temperature and rainfall, or investigating the cogwheels in a bicycle can provide data or starting points for discussion in your mathematics lessons as well as opportunities to apply and use mathematics in real contexts. (DfEE, 1999b: 16)

Unfortunately these sentiments did not seem to be reinforced in the detail of the framework and its yearly programmes, so that when the Primary Strategy was reviewed, it was necessary to point out the following.

> Within the curriculum, teachers and schools have the freedom to decide … how to arrange learning in the school day. There is no requirement for subjects to be taught discretely – they can be grouped, or taught through projects – if strong enough links are created between subjects, pupils' knowledge and skills can be used across the whole curriculum. (DfES, 2003: following para. 2.39)

Significantly, the revised Primary Strategy in England now includes as one of its key principles: 'greater momentum in literacy and mathematics across the primary phase with increased flexibility to secure links across the curriculum' (DfES, 2006a: 1).

From the perspective of the mathematics educator, the importance of cross-curricular links involving mathematics has three aspects.

Using and applying mathematics in other subjects

Other curriculum areas can provide opportunities to serve the aim of using and applying mathematics and to do this through purposeful activities. Historically, much of the content of mathematics as a subject was developed to solve practical problems in science, economics, the social sciences, and other fields of human endeavour. The nature of the subject therefore makes it almost obligatory that in learning to use and apply mathematics – one of the key attainment targets in the curriculum – pupils at all stages should use their mathematical skills and knowledge in other subjects. This will almost certainly happen anyway, to some extent – it is difficult to do much science, for example, without using some mathematics – but there is perhaps a need for teachers to plan the application of mathematical skills and knowledge in a more deliberate way. For example, a primary teacher teaching a Year 6 class (10 to 11 years) how to calculate and use percentages could plan opportunities to use these skills in, say, whatever geography project or history topic is being taught concurrently.

Meaningful contexts for learning mathematics

Other curriculum areas can provide meaningful contexts within which to introduce and develop mathematical concepts and skills. New mathematical material does not have to be introduced in a mathematics lesson. Primary school teachers with responsibility for delivering most of the curriculum to one class are uniquely placed to adopt a flexible approach to introducing new mathematical material that exploits the meaningful contexts of practical work across the curriculum. For example, the mathematics involved in timing events, measuring and recording time intervals, and using timing devices such as stopwatches or stop-clocks, could be taught entirely through activities with a high level of purposefulness within physical education and cookery lessons.

Cross-curricular projects

There is also some encouragement in current policy statements for primary teachers to adopt an even more flexible approach to delivering the curriculum, in which pupils engage in an extended project not linked to any particular curriculum subject, but drawing on all areas of the curriculum and developing creativity, generic thinking skills and problem-solving strategies. For example, pupils might tackle problems such as, 'How do we make the playground a better place for children?' or 'How can we improve lunch at school?' In such projects, mathematical skills are inevitably involved in realistic and relevant activity; and there is potential for pupils to see mathematics as something that can be used to 'make things happen' (Haylock et al., 1985).

PRACTICAL EXAMPLES

A further example of each of the first two aspects of cross-curricular mathematics discussed above is given below.

Applying number skills in physical education and English

A teacher in Key Stage 1 is planning to teach pupils to order a set of single-digit and 2-digit numbers and position them on a number line. Simultaneously, opportunities to use these skills are planned in other curriculum activities.

In a physical education lesson pupils will play a game that ends up with each member of each team of eight holding a card with a 2-digit number written on it: the winning team is the first team to line up with the numbers in order from smallest to largest.

In an English session looking at favourite story books, in the context of discussing whether children prefer long or short stories, each group of pupils will have the task of arranging a collection of popular story books in order, according to how many pages they have.

Learning data handling skills in other subjects

A teacher in Key Stage 2 decides that over the year everything that has to be taught about data handling can be done outside of mathematics lessons. Some practical work in science on measuring temperatures as substances cool will be used to teach pupils about line graphs; this will be reinforced in looking at the differing rates of growth of bean plants under various conditions. Frequency tables and bar charts will be taught in geography in surveys to be undertaken in a local study project; this material will be reinforced in a survey about favourite authors in English lessons and in collecting data from timing pupils in various activities in physical education. This data will also be used to introduce the concept of range as used in statistics.

FURTHER READING

Chapter 5 of Turner and McCullogh (2004) has plenty of practical suggestions for cross-curricular mathematics. Section 3 of the 1995 Yearbook of the US National Council of Teachers of Mathematics (NCTM, 1995) has a number of very relevant entries dealing specifically with connections across the elementary school curriculum.

RELATED ENTRY

Aims of mathematics teaching. Meaningful context. Purposeful activity. Using and applying mathematics.

Deductive and Inductive Reasoning

DEFINITION

There are two kinds of reasoning that feature prominently in doing mathematics. Inductive reasoning is the kind of thinking involved in recognizing patterns, similarities and equivalences, and using these to predict further results and to formulate generalizations. Deductive reasoning is the formulation of a valid, logical argument to explain, demonstrate or convince others that a solution to a problem must be correct, or that a mathematical theorem is proved beyond doubt, or that a particular conjecture is true or false.

EXPLANATION AND DISCUSSION

Observing from a number of examples that the product of an odd number and an even number always gives an even number and formulating this as a generalization ('odd multiplied by even gives even') is an example of inductive reasoning. To prove that it must necessarily always be the case that the product of an odd number and an even number must be even would be a typically mathematical way of reasoning deductively. But even to argue that, for example, '67 × 48 = 3261' must be incorrect because 67 is odd, 48 is even and 3261 is odd, and we know that an odd number multiplied by an even number cannot give an odd number, is to begin to reason deductively.

The National Curriculum for England (DfEE, 1999a) contains elements of both inductive and deductive reasoning in the programmes of study for Key Stage (KS)1 (5 to 7 years) and KS2 (7 to 11 years) mathematics. In terms of inductive reasoning, for example, pupils should be taught to:

- recognize simple patterns and relationships and make predictions about them (DfEE, 1999a, KS1: 65);
- understand and investigate general statements; search for pattern in their results (DfEE, 1999a, KS2: 67).

In terms of deductive reasoning, pupils should be taught to:

- explain their methods and reasoning when solving problems (DfEE, 1999a, KS1: 62);
- develop logical thinking and explain their reasoning (DfEE, 1999a, KS2: 67);
- use mathematical reasoning to explain features of shape and space (DfEE, 1999a, KS2: 71).

This recognition of the importance of learning to reason mathematically is reinforced in the revised Primary Strategy (DfES, 2006b: 9), which states that 'children need to be taught how to describe, interpret and explain what they see and how to use this as a basis to inform their thinking and reasoning'. Learning to think mathematically involves 'making deductions on the basis of given information ....' 'Reasoning' is one of the five themes in the *Using and Applying Mathematics* strand in this revised mathematics framework. However, the focus in this theme seems to be mainly on inductive reasoning, reflecting the fact that this is likely to be more significant than deductive reasoning for pupils in this age range learning mathematics. For example, pupils in Year 2 (6 to 7 years) will 'describe patterns and relationships with numbers and shapes, make predictions and test these with examples'; and pupils in Year 5 (9 to 10 years) will 'propose a general statement involving numbers or shapes and identify examples for which the statement is true or false' (DfES, 2006b: 4–5). These ideas are discussed more fully in this book in the entries for Equivalence, Generalization and Principle Learning.

Deductive reasoning in its most powerful form is used when we provide a proof of a mathematical result or theorem. For example, in geometry, having measured the angles in many examples of isosceles triangles, we may reason by induction, that 'if two sides of a triangle are equal in length, then the two angles opposite these sides must be equal.' But a mathematician would still require a proof that this must always be the case. Such a proof would consist of a valid, logical argument leading step by step from what is given about the triangle (the 'if' part of the statement) to the conclusion (the 'then' part).

Formal mathematical proof is certainly beyond most pupils in primary schools, but this does not mean that there is no place for deductive reasoning. Pupils in this age range can begin to formulate explanations for why things must work, to attempt to convince others why a mathematical result must be true, and to make a start in using the language of deductive reasoning. The 'communicating' theme in the *Using and Applying Mathematics* strand of the Primary Framework (DfES, 2006b: 4–5) suggests that pupils in Year 2 (6 to 7 years) should 'explain decisions, methods and results', pupils in Year 4 (8 to 9 years) should 'report solutions to puzzles and problems, giving explanations and reasoning' and pupils in Year 6 (10 to 11 years) should 'explain reasoning and conclusions'.

PRACTICAL EXAMPLES

Three examples are given below: two showing how primary pupils might begin to provide a convincing explanation for a generalization; the other focusing on the language of logic.

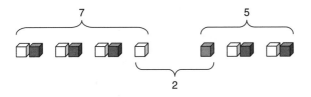

Figure 10 *The sum of two odd numbers is an even number*

Giving a convincing explanation

A Year 6 pupil may have used inductive reasoning in relation to Figure 14 (see Generalization) to determine the general rule for how many sticks are required to build a chain of hexagons. It is quite feasible that the pupil could be encouraged to go further than this and to reason more deductively to formulate a convincing explanation as to how you can be sure that this rule will always work; along these lines: 'There's this one stick you need to start with, then every time you add another hexagon you need five more sticks. So that's the number of hexagons multiplied by five, plus one.'

Similarly, with guidance from the teacher, a Year 4 pupil might be able to use blocks, as illustrated with 7 + 5 in Figure 10, to reason deductively why it is that the sum of two odd numbers is always an even number: 'When you have an odd number of blocks and put them in twos, there's always one left over. You can use the two leftover blocks to make another pair, so it must be an even number.'

Logical connectives

Particularly important in developing the ability to reason deductively is confidence in using what are called 'logical connectives' in mathematical statements. These are the little words – 'and', 'or', 'but', 'neither', 'nor', 'if … then …' – that we use to connect together statements and clauses. The most common form of logically invalid argument is to confuse 'if *A* then *B*' with its converse, 'if *B* then *A*'. For example, this statement about four-sided figures is true: 'If it is a square then the diagonals will cross at right angles.' But the converse statement is false: 'If it has diagonals crossing at right angles then it is a square.' (Consider a rhombus that is not a square.) Primary pupils can develop their use of these important logical connectives in formulating precise mathematical statements through sorting and set diagrams. For example, using Figure 11, a set of whole numbers from 1 to 50 could be sorted using two overlapping sets, with the attributes

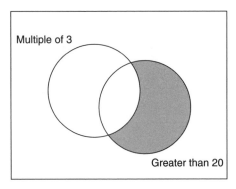

Whole numbers 1–50

Figure 11 *Sorting numbers using two attributes*

'multiple of 3' and 'greater than 20'. Pupils would then be asked to identify where in the diagram they would find numbers that are:

- a multiple of 3 and greater than 20 (such as 27);
- not a multiple of 3 but greater than 20 (such as 28);
- a multiple of 3 but not greater than 20 (such as 18);
- a multiple of 3 or greater than 20 or both (such as 6, 23 and 24);
- a multiple of 3 or greater than 20 but not both (such as 6 and 23);
- neither a multiple of 3 nor greater than 20 (such as 17).

Then, if all the numbers in one of the four subsets in Figure 11 (for example, those in the shaded area) are removed, pupils can be asked if the following statements are true or false about the numbers remaining in the diagram:

- if a number is a multiple of 3 then it is greater than 20;
- if a number is greater than 20 then it is a multiple of 3;
- if a number is not a multiple of 3 then it is not greater than 20;
- if a number is not greater than 20 then it is not a multiple of 3.

(The second and third statements are true; the other two are false.)

FURTHER READING

There is a good section on inductive and deductive (as well as intuitive) reasoning in Baroody (1993: 57–72), with some interesting examples of problems designed to develop logical reasoning in pupils in this age range. You might also read chapter 27 on mathematical reasoning in Haylock (2006). Pound (2006) provides useful guidance for promoting mathematical reasoning in younger children. Hejny and Slezáková provide some interesting case studies of young children's mathematical reasoning (chapter 5 in Cockburn, 2007).

RELATED ENTRIES

Aims of mathematics teaching. Equivalence. Generalization. Principle learning.

Differentiation

DEFINITION

In relation to teaching in primary schools, the term 'differentiation' refers to ways in which teachers take into account in their planning and teaching the differences between the pupils in the class. A definition provided by the Scottish Office Education Department is as follows.

> Differentiation is the identification of, and effective provision for, a range of abilities in one classroom, such that pupils in a particular class need not study the same thing at the same pace and in the same way at all times. Differentiated approaches should mean that the needs of the very able, and of children with learning difficulties, are discerned and met. (Simpson and Ure, 1994: 1)

EXPLANATION AND DISCUSSION

In mathematics, differences between pupils in a year group in terms of their levels of attainment or competence with key knowledge and skills are often more marked than in other subjects. For example, in a typical group of 7-year-olds some pupils will be able to double any 2-digit number mentally, whereas others may not be able to confidently recall the doubles of some single-digit numbers. An often quoted finding, from the Cockcroft Report (Cockcroft, 1982), is that at age 11 there is in mathematics a 'seven-year gap': meaning that the level of mathematical achievement of an average 11-year-old is matched by that of some 7-year-olds and matches that of some 14-year-olds. This range of attainment inevitably has implications for the way in which teachers plan to match what pupils do in mathematics lessons to their individual levels of competence.

Other differences can have a significant impact on how pupils respond to particular learning tasks. Tomlinson (2000), for example, suggests that the need for differentiation in teaching is based on the belief that 'students who are the same age differ in their readiness to learn, their interests, their style of learning, their experiences and their life circumstances'. In a classic study of mathematical ability in school children, Krutetskii (1976) found that some pupils have a preference to represent mathematical problems in visual imagery, whereas others have a preference for representation in mathematical symbols. This difference between pupils may make certain kinds of explanation more or less helpful for different pupils. Another example of differences between pupils, familiar to any primary teacher, is reading competence. In a typical class of Year 3 pupils (aged 7 to 8 years), there will be some pupils who are fluent, independent readers, while others can have significant difficulty in reading texts without assistance. This range of competence in reading will have an effect, for example, on the way the teacher plans to communicate mathematical tasks to various groups of pupils and how they use textbooks or other written material to promote their learning.

The degree of differentiation required in teaching is clearly inversely proportional to the range of mathematical attainment within the class. In a larger primary school, where pupils in a year group are organized into a number of sets for mathematics based on levels of attainment, differentiation is less of an issue. By contrast the need for differentiation is particularly acute in small primary schools, where teachers may typically have pupils from two or three year groups in one class. One of the authors of this book taught a class of 16 children in a small rural primary school that contained pupils from each of the four year-groups in Key Stage 2 (ages 7 to 11 years). The gap between what the least able Year

3 pupil and the most able Year 6 pupil could do was huge. In this situation there was no real alternative to setting individual activities and targets for each pupil for every mathematics lesson.

Before the implementation of the National Numeracy Strategy in primary schools in England, a common method of organizing mathematics learning, particularly in Key Stage 2, was for each pupil to work individually through a commercial scheme at their own rate. This was an extreme form of differentiation, sometimes called 'differentiation by rate of progress'. It was justified by teachers arguing that they were responding to the individual needs and diversity of the pupils in their classes. However, in practice, this approach was found to be ineffective and was repeatedly criticized by government inspectors and mathematics educators. For example, Haylock (1991: 44–7) identified shortcomings in this approach as being: an over-reliance on the written text as the medium of instruction; insufficient opportunity for teacher explanation of key mathematical concepts and processes; pupils wasting time queuing at the teacher's desk; omission of practical work because of the difficulties of organizing the resources required; and paucity of pupil–pupil talk about mathematical tasks.

Not surprisingly, in this context, the National Numeracy Strategy brought a return to a much greater emphasis on whole-class teaching. It is much more common now in primary mathematics lessons in England to see teachers engaging with the whole class in direct interactive teaching than to see a teacher sitting at a desk with a queue of pupils waiting for attention. However, there is still an acknowledgement of the need for some form of differentiation. One of the principles underpinning the National Numeracy Strategy was 'controlled differentiation'. Teachers were encouraged to 'ensure that differentiation is manageable and centred around work common to all pupils in a class, with targeted, positive support to help those who have difficulties with mathematics to keep up with their peers' (DfEE, 1999b: 5).

Tomlinson (2000) argues that an emphasis on standards-based teaching does not remove the need for the teacher to be sensitive to the differentiated needs of their pupils. Indeed, in reporting on mathematics in primary schools, the Chief Inspector of Schools in England (Ofsted, 2005, downloadable from live.ofsted.gov.uk/publications) observed that 'the most successful teachers interpret the lesson structure with due consideration of the needs of the pupils … good use is made of targeted questions and differentiated learning activities'.

PRACTICAL EXAMPLES

Some examples of the different ways in which differentiation might be achieved in teaching mathematics in primary schools are given below.

Differentiation by task

In this approach to differentiation, pupils in different ability groups are assigned different tasks, matched to the ability of the group. The guidance for the Numeracy Strategy recommended that when teachers are working with groups they should keep the number of groups to a maximum of four, so that supporting the groups is manageable. It further recommended that the tasks provided for these groups should be on a common theme and at no more than three levels of difficulty (DfEE, 1999b). The advantage of setting these tasks within one shared theme is that this gives opportunities for the skilful teacher to engage in some whole-class interactive teaching around the theme. A further important strategy for the teacher is to ensure that only one of the tasks is particularly demanding of teacher input. For example, part of one lesson in a series on doubling could be structured like this: the least able group could be assigned to play a self-correcting card game that involves matching single-digit numbers to their doubles; the two middle-ability groups might work through some exercises in the textbook reinforcing their skills in doubling numbers up to 50; and the teacher could focus on an interactive session with the more able group, extending their doubling skills to numbers over 100.

Differentiation in questioning

In introducing the tasks on doubling described above, the teacher might have had a whole-class question-and-answer session about doubling, making use of differentiation in questioning. For example, in exploring how some doubles can be usefully related to multiples of 5, the teacher might direct a question about using this idea to double 7 to a less able pupil, and then direct a similar question about doubling 47 to a more able pupil.

Differentiation by outcome

This approach is essentially to give pupils the same task, but to expect different outcomes in terms of what is achieved. For example, a class might be given a sheet of graduated mathematics questions and some pupils told that they only have to do the first section, while others are told they have to do them all. In general this is not a particularly sensitive or effective approach in mathematics.

Differentiation by enrichment and extension

A modification of differentiation by outcome is an approach in which initially all pupils do essentially the same basic tasks, but then pupils are given supplementary tasks chosen with their differing needs in mind. These are designed to broaden or extend their experience of using and applying their mathematical skills and knowledge. This is an effective approach for meeting the needs of more able pupils in mathematics.

FURTHER READING

The findings of a project that reviewed how schools interpreted and implemented differentiation policies are reported in Weston et al. (1998). Using case studies, a national survey and published material, this report shows the major shifts in expectations of pupils' achievements during the 1990s and how schools have responded to the challenge of meeting the needs of all pupils. Jones and Allebone provide a helpful chapter on differentiation (in Koshy et al., 2000). A recommendation for those who teach younger children is chapter 17 on managing differentiation, in Edwards (1998).

RELATED ENTRIES

Explanation. Match and mismatch. Questioning

differentiation

Equivalence

DEFINITION

'Equivalent' is the technical mathematical term that corresponds to the everyday language, 'is the same as'. In learning mathematics, children often encounter situations in which they have to recognize that all the things in a given set are in some sense 'the same'. In doing this they have therefore identified an equivalence. This process of recognizing samenesses in sets of mathematical entities is an important way of thinking in mathematics.

EXPLANATION AND DISCUSSION

Recognizing similarities and differences is a fundamental cognitive process by means of which we organize and make sense of our experiences. This process is significant in most fields of human activity, from social interaction to science. It has a particular application in learning mathematics, in terms of equivalence (what is the same?) and transformation (what is different?). Some examples will demonstrate how widespread is the concept of equivalence in the experience of children learning mathematics, both in terms of conceptual learning and as a tool for manipulating mathematical ideas.

In the early stages of number, children learn to recognize that there is something the same about, say, a set of three chocolates and a set of three teddy bears. These two collections are different from each other (teddy bears are different from chocolates), but there is something very significantly the same about them. They are both described by the adjective 'three', which describes a property they share. The fact that they share this property of 'threeness' can be shown by one-to-one matching, a dynamic experience for the young child that makes what is the same about three chocolates and three teddy bears explicit. The property that makes these two sets equivalent is then abstracted from many collections of three things to form the concept of 'three' as a cardinal number, existing in its own right, independent of any specific context.

This example illustrates how many abstract mathematical concepts are formed by identifying equivalences, recognizing things that are the same or properties that are shared. Geometry provides many such examples. In learning the concept of 'square', for example, children may engage in sorting a set of two-dimensional shapes that includes a number of squares of different sizes. When they put together all the squares into a subset, because they are 'all the same shape', they are using reasoning on the basis of equivalence. The shapes are not all the same, of course, because they may differ in size or colour, for example. But they are all the same in some sense; they share a property; there is an equivalence.

This is one reason why this kind of thinking is so powerful and fundamental to mathematics. It enables learners to hold in their mind one conceptual idea (such as 'three' or 'square') which is an abstraction of their experiences of many specific examples of the concept, all of which are in some sense the same, all of which are equivalent in this respect. In doing this, the learner combines a number of individual experiences of specific exemplars, which have been recognized as being the same in some sense, into one abstraction.

An equivalence relation when applied to a set of mathematical entities partitions that set into a number of subsets, within which the items are 'equivalent', that is, they share a mathematical property. For example, if children investigate the remainders that arise when the integers from 1 to 20 are divided by 3, they find there are three subsets, with numbers that give remainders 0, 1 and 2:

1. $\{3, 6, 9, 12, 15, 18\}$;
2. $\{1, 4, 7, 10, 13, 16, 19\}$;
3. $\{2, 5, 8, 11, 14, 17, 30\}$.

Within each of these three subsets the numbers have a shared property.

1. They are all multiples of 3.
2. They are all 1 more than a multiple of 3.
3. They are all 2 more than a multiple of 3.

Technically, the three subsets are called 'equivalence classes' (Williams and Shuard, 1994: 495–7). In learning mathematics, children often sort mathematical entities into equivalence classes. For example, sorting a set of two-dimensional shapes into those with the same numbers of sides generates these equivalence classes: triangles, quadrilaterals, pentagons, hexagons, and so on.

The concept of equivalence is also powerful as a mathematical tool. If two mathematical objects are regarded in some sense as the same, then, in appropriate circumstances, one member of an equivalence class can be replaced by any other. For example, fractions can be sorted into sets of equivalent fractions, such as $\{^1/_4, \, ^2/_8, \, ^3/_{12}, \, ^4/_{16}, \, \dots \}$ The fraction $^2/_8$ is not in every sense the same as the fraction $^1/_4$: one piece of a cake cut into four equal parts is not identical in every respect to two pieces of the cake cut into 8 equal parts. However, it is the same amount of cake. There is an equivalence here, which pupils have to learn to recognize – and then to use. For example, when adding $^3/_8$ to $^1/_4$, it is appropriate and helpful to be able to replace the $^1/_4$ by the equivalent fraction $^2/_8$.

Primary school teachers should therefore be aware of the importance of promoting this kind of thinking in pupils, getting them to identify and to use equivalences. Every opportunity should be taken to ask the basic question, 'What is the same?' Pupils should be asked to look at pairs or larger collections of numbers, shapes and other mathematical entities and identify ways in which they are the same, or to sort them into subsets of items that share some property. Alongside this, pupils can be asked to say in what ways two numbers, shapes or objects are different: this task engages the pupil in the corresponding process of transformation.

PRACTICAL EXAMPLES

Four examples below illustrate the prevalence of the concept of equivalence in primary mathematics.

One–one matching

Young children are given one-to-one matching experience by setting a table for six people, with each place-setting having one knife, one fork, one plate, one cup, one saucer, one spoon. The teacher and children together count how many of each item there are on the table, and then arrange them in different ways to make the matching explicit. The teacher repeatedly uses phrases such as 'one of these for one of those' and 'the number of these is the same as the number of those'.

Shapes: What's my rule?

The teacher and a group of children look together at a set of three-dimensional geometric shapes. The teacher tells the children that there is a rule for sorting these shapes. If a shape satisfies the rule it goes into the 'yes' group, otherwise into the 'no' group. After a few examples of shapes being placed into one or other of the two groups, the children are asked to predict whether the remaining shapes are yes or no. When the sorting is completed, the children are asked to say what is the same about all the shapes; what is the rule the teacher has used? This is repeated with different rules. Then the children may have the opportunity to use their own rules to sort the shapes. Each time this is done the 'yes' group demonstrates an equivalence. For example, if the rule used is 'all the angles are right angles', then the set of equivalent shapes selected is the set of cuboids.

Numbers: What's my rule?

This is a similar activity with integers (whole numbers). The teacher asks the children to suggest numbers and then writes these on the board in either the 'yes' set or the 'no' set. The children have to guess the rule and say what is the same about all the numbers in the 'yes' set. Examples of rules might be 'between 9 and 100' (the set of 2-digit numbers) or 'the final digit is 6 or 1' (all these numbers are 1 more than a multiple of 5).

What is the same?

Pupils are given two shapes (such as those in Figure 12) or two numbers (such as 16 and 36) and invited to find as many ways as they can in which the two numbers or shapes are the same. They formulate sentences beginning with the words, 'they both … ' or 'they are both … '. For example, for the shapes, 'they both have four sides'. Or, for the numbers, 'they are both square numbers'.

Figure 12 *What is the same about these two shapes?*

FURTHER READING

Equivalence is one of the central themes of Haylock and Cockburn (2003), featuring particularly in chapter 7 in their analysis of children's learning about shape and space.

RELATED ENTRIES

Concept learning. Transformation.

Errors

DEFINITION

Pupils make errors in mathematics in their written work, in practical tasks, and in their oral responses to teachers' questions. Errors can be the result of carelessness or procedural slips. More significant, however, are those errors that reveal misunderstandings of mathematical concepts, procedures and principles. Teachers can respond to these positively as a source of evidence that will help them to improve their teaching and as a means of promoting more secure learning in their pupils.

EXPLANATION AND DISCUSSION

Pupils in primary schools probably make more errors in mathematics than in any other aspect of the curriculum, apart perhaps from spelling. The reason for this is that, like spelling, most of the tasks that pupils are given in mathematics require responses that will be judged as either right or wrong. Pupils have to learn that getting things right in mathematics is important. The nature of the subject is that accuracy is a sine qua non when we use and apply mathematics in practice. None of us wants to be treated by a nurse who confuses millilitres and centilitres, or, when exchanging currency, to be served by someone who chooses the wrong calculation and offers us 72 euros for £100. So, how does a teacher respond to errors made by pupils in a mathematics lesson, whether in written work, practical tasks such as measurement, or in oral responses to the teacher's questions? Reminding pupils of the importance of taking care and being accurate in their work is one response. This is sometimes justifiable and necessary, particularly in relation to careless errors in written work and practical tasks. Other errors are just minor processing errors, which may be little more than a slip in carrying out a mathematical procedure arising from a momentary lapse in concentration. In such cases the teacher's role is no more than to point out the error and to leave it to the pupil to make the necessary correction. But there are many times when a more positive response to errors in mathematics is more appropriate: because teachers actually need pupils to make some errors, particularly those that reveal real misunderstandings about mathematical concepts, procedures and principles. There are four dimensions to a more positive approach to pupils' errors in mathematics.

Challenging and matching

First, if every pupil every time gave correct responses to every task we gave them in mathematics then we would have to question seriously whether we were challenging our pupils sufficiently. Teachers need their pupils to make some errors to indicate that the tasks they are giving them are providing sufficient challenge. Of course, if a pupil gets wrong a large proportion of the questions they are given in mathematics, then the most significant conclusion from this evidence is not that the pupil lacks ability in the subject (although they might) but that the teacher is doing a poor job in matching the tasks to the pupil's level of competence.

Insights into misunderstandings

Second, teachers can make use of pupils' errors to gain insights into the pupils' misunderstandings and confusions. These insights help the teacher to teach mathematics with more awareness of potential difficulties. For example, a 9-year-old pupil gives the answer 127 to the calculation 340 – 227. The teacher is keen to diagnose the nature of this error and asks the pupil to explain how the subtraction was done. The pupil's response includes the 'explanation' that 'if you take seven away from nothing then it's still seven.' Analysing this misunderstanding the teacher recognizes that part of the problem is the use of the word 'nothing' for 'zero' – so, because it is nothing, it can just be ignored. This insight is really helpful for the teacher both in addressing this pupil's misunderstanding and in the teacher's future teaching about how to handle zeros in calculations. This example illustrates the importance of following up potentially significant errors in written work with discussion, oral questions and opportunities for pupils to provide their own explanations.

Promoting learning

Third, an error made by a pupil can be seen as a positive opportunity to promote learning. This attitude to errors is consistent with the approach of assessment for learning (Black, 2003). Learning from our mistakes is often the most effective form of learning in mathematics, particularly if the teacher can make use of cognitive conflict. For example, the teacher faced with the subtraction error above could begin by presenting the pupil with the subtraction $10 - 7$, confident that the pupil will know that this is equal to 3; then follow this with a series of subtractions, such as $20 - 7$, $30 - 7$, $40 - 7$, $140 - 7$, and so on, until the pupil is able to respond correctly to $340 - 7$. The teacher can then ask the pupil to look again at the response to $340 - 227$. Seeing these two calculations side by side is likely to cause cognitive conflict in the pupil's mind, which the pupil may now be able to resolve by correcting the original error. If this proves to be the case then the resulting learning will be much more secure than if the teacher had simply explained why the answer was wrong and repeated the correct procedure.

Classroom ethos

Fourth, it is possible for a primary school teacher to generate a classroom ethos in which errors and misunderstandings made by individual pupils are welcomed as an opportunity for the whole class to improve their understanding. In such a classroom a pupil making an error that reveals a mathematical difficulty or possible misunderstanding is seen as a helpful occurrence for the whole class. The teacher may even thank the pupil for making the error, because of the opportunity it provides for all the pupils to learn from it and to be aware of a potential pitfall. In such an approach the teacher does not seek at all costs to teach in a way that minimizes pupil error, but will allow errors to occur, sometimes quite deliberately. Clearly, such an approach requires sensitivity on the part of the teacher and awareness that there are some pupils who find it very difficult to be seen to make mistakes. But this approach has been endorsed by the Office for Standards in Education (Ofsted), the government's inspection agency in England, who found that effective teachers 'cultivate an ethos where pupils do not mind making mistakes because errors are seen as part of the learning' (Ofsted, 2003: para. 35).

PRACTICAL EXAMPLES

Two examples of common errors and the teachers' responses to them are described below.

A procedural error in addition

A 5-year-old doing additions by counting on makes the same error repeatedly, with responses such as: $7 + 3 = 9$, $6 + 5 = 10$ and $8 + 4 = 11$.

The teacher asks the pupil to show how these answers were obtained and notices that in doing the addition of 3 to 7, the pupil counts 'seven, eight, nine', while turning up three fingers in turn. The pupil is 'counting on 3 from 7' but incorrectly starting at the 7. The teacher recalls similar errors that some pupils made when doing additions by counting on along a number line. Analysis of the errors leads the teacher to modify the teaching of these procedures, using the language 'seven and three more' rather than 'seven, count on three'. This is immediately effective, so the teacher reinforces this particular language pattern in subsequent oral work with the whole class.

Misunderstanding a rule for multiplication by 10

A teacher notices that a number of pupils in a class of 11-year-olds in some written exercises give the incorrect result, $2.3 \times 10 = 2.30$. The teacher takes this as an opportunity to promote deeper understanding with all the pupils, asking the class how they thought this answer had been obtained. It transpires that the error arose because pupils had been misapplying a 'rule' for multiplying by ten, namely, 'add a zero'. The teacher asks the pupils which is the bigger number, 2.3 or 2.30? This provokes a lively discussion, leading to general agreement that they are the same, and raising questions about the rule. This sows the first seeds of cognitive conflict in pupils' minds. The teacher then asks the class to suggest a situation in real life that might correspond to the multiplication 2.3×10. One pupil suggests buying 10 planks of wood, each 2.3 metres long, and finding the total length. Another suggests buying 2.3 kg of chocolate at £10 per kilogram. Connecting the multiplication in symbols with these real-life situations generates more cognitive conflict, which is quickly resolved. The new insights obtained by pupils are then quickly reinforced by discussion of further examples, which are also connected with real-life situations. Finally, the teacher thanks the pupils who made the original error for helping the class to understand the mathematics better.

errors

FURTHER READING

Cockburn (1999) deals with the identification, diagnosis and remediation of young children's mathematical errors. Drews provides a helpful overview of children's mathematical errors and misconceptions (chapter 2 in Hansen, 2005). The rest of Hansen (2005) provides a comprehensive analysis of children's errors across the mathematics curriculum. Also worth reading is Koshy's chapter on 'Children's mistakes and misconceptions' (in Koshy et al., 2000).

RELATED ENTRIES

Assessment for learning. Cognitive conflict. Gender and mathematics. Match and mismatch.

Explanation

DEFINITION

Explanation is a key teaching skill through which teachers help pupils to understand mathematical tasks, objectives, procedures, concepts, principles and relationships. In a key text on the skill of explaining, Wragg and Brown (2001a: 6) provide the following operational definition: 'Explaining is giving understanding to another.' Pupils can also participate in providing explanations in a mathematics classroom, but in this entry we focus on teachers doing the explaining.

EXPLANATION AND DISCUSSION

Haylock (2006: 1) argues that 'one of the best ways for children to learn and to understand much of the mathematics in the primary school curriculum is for a teacher who understands it to explain it to them'. Children agree. Research into what children think makes a good teacher indicates consistently that children like teachers who explain things clearly (Wragg, 1984).

Promoting the importance of explanation as a teaching skill in mathematics is not inconsistent with a constructivist approach to teaching and learning. The teacher's explanations can be part of the experience that helps pupils to construct their own understanding of mathematical experiences. Often this involves helping the pupil to reflect on all they have been experiencing in mathematical exploration and to identify what is significant and how it connects with other experiences and their existing understanding. Skilful explanation will always involve the use of questioning to ascertain the extent to which the pupil has the necessary understanding of various mathematical ideas already in place. So, teachers explaining can go hand-in-hand with pupils learning through investigation and discovery. For example, the pupil might construct their own understanding of subtraction with 3-digit numbers through explorations of price comparisons using 1p, 10p and £1 coins, but then the teacher can build on this through careful explanation of the procedure for subtraction by decomposition.

By definition, good explanation always seeks to promote understanding. So, effective explanation will use examples and non-examples, illustrations, and analogies. It will put abstract mathematical ideas into a variety of contexts and seek to enable the pupil to make connections. It will help pupils, for example, to connect the manipulation of mathematical symbols with concrete materials, pictures and both informal and formal mathematical language. It is important that explanation should not be conceived just in terms of the teacher talking. In mathematics pupils need simple diagrams to shape their thinking; and important numbers and key words should be written on the board to help pupils remember the details of the explanation.

Wragg and Brown (2001a: 7–9) identify some features of effective explanation, three of which are discussed below.

Using a key idea or principle

A key idea or principle can help unlock understanding. For example, in explaining the process of 'carrying one' in addition a key idea that would be used and reinforced repeatedly would be the principle of place value: that as you move right to left along the digits in a multidigit number, 'ten of these can be exchanged for one of these' (Haylock, 2006: 57).

Use of the voice

Variation in the use of the voice, with light and shade, emphasis and gesture, is a key ingredient of successful explanation. Emphasis and rhythm are particularly important in helping pupils to be aware of pattern in mathematics. For example, to help children recognize the 'principle of complements' (Haylock and Cockburn, 2003: 113), the teacher might deliver a sequence of questions in the following way, emphasizing the words in italics: 'Ten subtract (opening right hand) *four* (pause) is (pointing to the left) *six* (pause), so ten subtract (opening left hand) *six* (pause, rising inflexion) must be (pointing to the right) ... ?'

Awareness of structure

In mathematics especially this is fundamental to effective explanation. Teachers must clarify before they start teaching the structure of the mathematical ideas involved: which ideas are dependent on which other ideas, and what is the most effective sequence of examples to use to ensure that the mathematical concepts, principles and procedures to be learnt will emerge clearly. One of the fundamental prerequisites for effective explanation is therefore that the teacher should have a secure understanding of the structure of the mathematical ideas they are teaching. Gifford (2005: 75) stresses, even for those teaching in the Foundation Stage (3 to 5 years), the 'importance of teachers knowing about the concepts, facts and skills of mathematical topics in order to help children to learn and to recognise when they are learning'.

PRACTICAL EXAMPLES

Primary school teachers might find themselves explaining mathematical tasks, objectives, procedures, concepts, principles, and relationships. The last three of these are dealt with elsewhere in this book, so here are some examples of the other kinds of explanations.

Explaining a task

A group of pupils aged 6–7 years, investigating capacity, is to be given the task of arranging a set of six containers in order from the smallest to the largest capacity, by pouring water from one to the other. Before they begin the teacher must explain the task. This will involve ensuring that the pupils understand and have to the fore in their minds the mathematical ideas involved: what is meant by the capacity of a container, the concept of ordering from smallest to largest, how you interpret what happens when you fill one container and pour its contents into another. It will involve making sure the pupils understand what they are trying to achieve and how they will present their results at the end. Getting a pupil to demonstrate a comparison of capacity with two containers, where it is not obvious as to which is the larger and which the smaller, will help the pupils to understand what the task is about.

Explaining an objective

At the start of any teaching session it is helpful for teachers to make explicit to pupils their learning objectives for the lesson. For example, the teacher might write on the board: 'Our target for today is to learn how to calculate near-doubles mentally.' To explain this objective the teacher will show how it links to what the pupils had been learning previously and use questioning to clarify the meaning of key words, such as 'calculate', 'doubles', 'near-doubles' and 'mentally'. The teacher will then give some examples of the kinds of things the pupils will be able to do at the end of the lesson if the objective has been achieved, such as 28 + 29 and 152 + 149, asking pupils to explain why these are near-doubles and then repeating their explanations with greater clarity.

Explaining a procedure

An important procedure for mental addition is that of bridging through multiples of 10. For example, when mentally adding 8 to 57 we might add 3 to get to 60 and then a further 5. To explain this procedure effectively a teacher would first rehearse with pupils: (a) counting in tens; and (b) the different ways in which 8 can be partitioned into two numbers. This gets the necessary prerequisite knowledge to the fore. They would then connect the procedure with some kind of visual imagery, such as a hundred-square, getting a pupil to show how, when you start at 57 on the square and count on 3, you get to 60 at the end of the row; and then counting on a further 5 gets you to 65. They would set the same procedure into a different context, such as adding 8 one-penny coins one at a time to 57p laid out in tens and ones, emphasizing with voice and gesture the moment when they pass through 60p. They would illustrate the procedure with several other examples. They would also show some non-examples (such as 53 + 4) to which this procedure does not apply and ask pupils why not.

FURTHER READING

A primary school teacher committed to improving the quality and effectiveness of their explanations in teaching mathematics might start with Haylock (2006), whose book aims 'to equip teachers with the knowledge they require to be able to explain mathematical ideas to their pupils with confidence' (p. 2). Otherwise, as will be clear from the

explanation

discussion above, the key book on the teaching skill of explanation is Wragg and Brown (2001a).

RELATED ENTRIES

Concept learning. Making connections. Principle learning. Questioning.

Gender and Mathematics

DEFINITION

In this entry, gender is considered in relation to those differences that might be observed or perceived between boys and girls in relation to learning mathematics. Gender differences are discussed in terms of achievement, attitudes, behaviour and equal opportunities.

EXPLANATION AND DISCUSSION

In the discussion that follows, it is important to understand that, whereas statistical trends may show some overall differences in achievement, attitudes and behaviours, individual pupils of both sexes are positioned right across the range.

Achievement

Girls tend to perform better overall in school than boys, but they perform less well than boys in mathematics. This observation could be interpreted as an issue about girls and mathematics. So, for example, research in the 1970s and 1980s focused on girls' relative under-achievement in mathematics, mainly at secondary level and in choosing to study mathematics post-16. Or it could be interpreted as an issue

Table 1 *Percentages of girls and boys achieving level 4 or above in the 2006 national tests in England for Year 6 pupils*

	Girls	Boys
English	85	74
Reading	87	79
Writing	75	59
Science	87	87
Maths	75	77

Source: www.dfes.gov.uk

Table 2 *Percentages of girls and boys achieving level 5 in the 2006 national tests in England for Year 6 pupils*

	Girls	Boys
English	39	26
Reading	53	41
Writing	23	13
Science	46	45
Maths	31	36

Source: www.dfes.gov.uk

about boys doing so poorly in most other subjects when compared to girls. So, current studies tend to focus on strategies to raise boys' achievement generally in school (see, for example, the University of Cambridge 'Raising Boys' Achievement Project', available at www-rba.educ.cam.ac.uk).

Tables 1 and 2 show the results for national tests in England taken in Year 6 (10 to 11 years) in 2006. Level 4 is the level that most pupils are expected to achieve at this age. The only subject in which boys do better than girls is mathematics. If this were a book about teaching English, then we would have to raise serious concerns about the poor performance of boys, particularly the worrying results for writing. In terms of mathematics, however, Table 1 shows that girls did less well than boys in the national tests and Table 2 shows that the difference was more marked at the higher level of achievement. Fewer girls achieve results that would put them in the category of high attainers in mathematics.

Attitudes

Joffe and Foxman (1986) gave questionnaires to 11–15-year-olds and found interesting gender differences concerning attitudes towards mathematics. Girls tended to be less confident about their mathematical performance and to underrate themselves, while boys tended to express greater expectations of success. These findings are echoed by Pomerantz et al. (2002). They suggest that we might expect that, because of their general academic success in school, girls would be more self-confident about their academic abilities and have higher academic self-esteem. They found, on the contrary, that girls are more likely to be overly critical in evaluating their own academic performance, whereas boys tend to overestimate their own academic abilities and accomplishments. Haylock (1984) found that among higher-attaining pupils aged 11 to 12 years the girls tended to show greater anxiety and a lower self-concept in mathematics than the boys. High anxiety and low self-concept correlated significantly with lower scores in tests of mathematical creativity. Pound (2006: 65–6) raises the issue of confidence in relation to younger children learning mathematics and reports that bright girls may be less resilient learners than boys; in other words, girls may be more inclined to give up in the face of difficulties.

Behaviour

Haylock (1984) found also that the girls in his sample were less inclined to take reasonable risks in unfamiliar mathematics tasks, tended to think in narrower categories and showed more rigidity in their thinking. Some writers note gender differences in mathematics and stereotypical behaviour appearing in boys and girls in the early years of schooling. Pound (2006: 132), discussing younger children learning mathematics, claims that 'girls, in particular, may enjoy keeping busy, doing unchallenging but safe activities, which frequently result in praise and rows of ticks'. Nutbrown (2006: 54–5) reports how in a nursery class a teacher noted that the children's choices of activity reflected their perception that the home area was for girls and the computer area for boys. Many teachers observe that boys will tend to dominate the use of computers and other practical equipment in mathematics classes, if children are left to their own devices. Gura (1992), however, found that stereotypical gender differences in the use of block play materials with young children disappeared if the adults became involved in the play and if the children were given sufficient time and space to explore the materials exhaustively.

All pupils need to have opportunities to work sometimes independently and sometimes collaboratively, as these are skills needed for later life and both kinds of experience contribute positively to mathematical development in different ways. Primary school teachers often observe that in general the girls in their class are better at working cooperatively than the boys. Girls are often better at sharing ideas, listening to one another and articulating their thoughts, an observation which may be associated with their greater language skills (see Tables 1 and 2). Boys, on the other hand, are often observed to be more competitive and will engage more positively in activities where there are winners and losers or where there is an opportunity to demonstrate their prowess.

Equal opportunities

It appears then that there is some evidence of gender-related differences in relation to achievement in mathematics, attitudes towards mathematics and behaviour in mathematical activities. What is not clear is the source of such differences. Young children will pick up views about mathematics and everything else that happens in school from their parents and from society generally. It may be the case that adults perpetuate an association between mathematics and those activities perceived as male, or the message is sent out that it is not important whether or not girls are good at mathematics. It is certainly the case that negative attitudes to mathematics can be passed on from one generation to another within families (Burnett and Wichman, 1997).

There is also a danger that teachers will treat boys and girls differently in mathematics classes because maybe unconsciously they actually believe that they are innately different or because the teachers themselves are influenced by the norms of society. For example, Soro (2002) reports that teachers in Finland showed strong beliefs that girls tend to rely on rote learning of routine procedures in mathematics and that boys demand and get more teacher attention. The perception was that girls are just hard workers, but boys use their brains. She raises the 'appalling' possibility that teachers who believe these things might reinforce and sustain these differences in their teaching. Teachers, particularly male teachers, are sometimes observed to be more protective towards girls in the way they deal with pupils' problems and errors in mathematics. Such behaviour by the teacher could serve to reinforce a non-risk-taking approach to problem solving in girls, while giving the boys the advantages of more opportunities to sort things out for themselves and thereby to construct their own meaning more securely.

PRACTICAL EXAMPLES

Clearly, primary school teachers cannot change society, but they can take measures to ensure that within their mathematics lessons they give equal opportunities to all pupils to achieve their potential. Some pointers for ensuring that neither boys nor girls are given more or less opportunity are suggested below. (See also the pointers provided in the entry for Anxiety about mathematics.)

1. Maintain a balance between cooperative, paired and individual work in mathematics lessons, in order not to favour particular groups who might do better in one or other of these.
2. Have mixed-sex groups for most activities, but be sensitive to groups being dominated by particular pupils, particularly when physical resources are involved; if necessary, have single-sex groups for some activities to ensure that all pupils get equal opportunity to access resources.
3. In any kind of collaborative work, be actively involved with groups and alert to any potential for lack of equal opportunity, or domination by particular pupils.
4. Avoid overemphasis on competition and speed of performance; never have competitions between boys and girls in mathematics.
5. Identify pupils who might be inclined towards a rote-learning set and, through questioning, positively encourage them to engage with understanding the mathematics they are doing and to seek to construct meaning; make this a goal for all pupils equally.
6. Monitor computer use and ensure that all children have equal access; for example, have a class tick list and a sand timer on the computer to ensure equal access for all.
7. Establish a classroom ethos in which the taking of reasonable risks is encouraged and in which there is a positive attitude towards pupils' errors.

8. Do not perpetuate gender-based perceptions about mathematics and other subjects in the school curriculum.
9. Do not make gender-related assumptions about how particular groups of pupils will respond or perform in mathematics.

FURTHER READING

A key text on ensuring gender equity in mathematics is Hanna (1996). Gallagher and Kaufman (2005) have put together a collection of writings, which indicates a renewed interest in this area; the book presents an integrated approach drawing on various branches of psychology, including cognitive, social, personality/self-oriented, and psychobiological. For data about gender differences in the achievements of gifted pupils in Britain and the USA, see Freeman (2003).

RELATED ENTRIES

Anxiety about mathematics. Creativity in mathematics. Errors. Talk.

Generalization

DEFINITION

Generalization is one of the fundamental and characteristic processes of thinking and reasoning mathematically. It is the process of recognizing and articulating what is always the case in a particular set of mathematical objects or relationships.

EXPLANATION AND DISCUSSION

In his influential research into the psychology of mathematical ability in school children, Krutetskii (1976: 350) identified the ability for rapid and broad generalization of mathematical objects, relations and operations as one of the key components that distinguishes pupils who are more able in mathematics from those who are less able. Krutetskii (1976: 237) identified two aspects of this ability: (a) the ability to recognize and apply in a specific situation a generalization that the pupil already knows; (b) the ability to see something general and as yet unknown to the pupil in one or more particular instances. In other words, pupils must learn both to apply the general to the particular and to deduce the general from the particular.

It is certainly the case that from their earliest years children use their awareness and response to pattern to formulate and use generalizations in mathematics. Indeed, they can only make progress in the subject by learning to generalize. For example, the process of counting beyond single-digit numbers relies on an awareness of the pattern of '… one, … two, … three …', which is repeated every ten numbers. Children recognize that this pattern will always occur and then use the generalization to go on counting with larger and larger numbers. Zoltan Dienes, a pioneer in the field of the psychology of learning mathematics, described this as 'extending the class of cases where a certain thing can be done from a finite to an infinite class' (Dienes, 1963: 98).

Pupils make or use generalizations whenever they use words such as 'always', 'each', 'every', 'all', 'never', 'forever'. For example, below are listed some of the ways in which children might generalize the pattern of squares in Figure 13.

- It *always* goes black, grey and then two white squares.
- *Each* grey square is followed by two white squares.
- *Every* time you get a black square you get a grey square next.
- *All* the grey squares follow black squares.
- The next square after a black square is *never* a white square.
- The pattern could continue black, grey, white, white, *forever*.

Effective teachers of mathematics in primary schools will encourage pupils to use words such as these to articulate their observations of

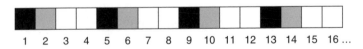

1 2 3 4 5 6 7 8 9 10 11 12 13 14 15 16 …

Figure 13 *A repeating pattern of squares*

pattern in mathematics and to make statements about what is always the case. Particularly important in formulating mathematical generaliza-tions is the language structure, 'if … then …', not least because it dis-tinguishes clearly between the two different assertions, 'if p then q' and 'if q then p'. For example, a correct generalization about multiples of 5 could be expressed as '*if* a whole number ends in a 5 *then* it is a multiple of 5'. The converse statement is an incorrect generalization: '*if* a whole number is a multiple of 5 *then* it ends in a 5'.

Because a generalization asserts what is always the case, it can be shown to be incorrect by the production of just one example where it is not the case. This is called a counter-example. For example, the number 20 is a counter-example for the generalization, 'if a whole number is a multiple of 5 then it ends in a 5'. It is a multiple of 5, but it does not end in a 5.

PRACTICAL EXAMPLES

Because forming generalizations is so fundamental to making progress in mathematics, primary school teachers will provide pupils with opportu-nities designed specifically to develop this kind of thinking.

Sequential and global generalizations

For example, pupils could be asked to number the squares shown in Figure 13, with 1, 2, 3, 4, … and so on, and then to investigate the sequence of numbers for the different shadings of squares. With the black squares, for example, pupils would investigate the pattern in this sequence of numbers: 1, 5, 9, 13, 17, … . The pattern here could be artic-ulated using a sequential generalization, such as: 'to get to the next black square you always count on 4'. Or it could be expressed more powerfully in a global generalization, such as: 'the numbers for black squares are always 1 more than a multiple of 4' (Haylock, 2006: 229–31).

Tabulation

One of the most effective approaches in the primary school is for pupils to tabulate results of investigations of patterns in sequences of numbers and shapes. For example, 6 sticks are needed to construct one hexagon. Figure 14 shows how 11, 16 and 21 sticks are needed to build chains of

Number of hexagons	Number of sticks
1	6
2	11
3	16
4	21
5	?
6	?
20	?

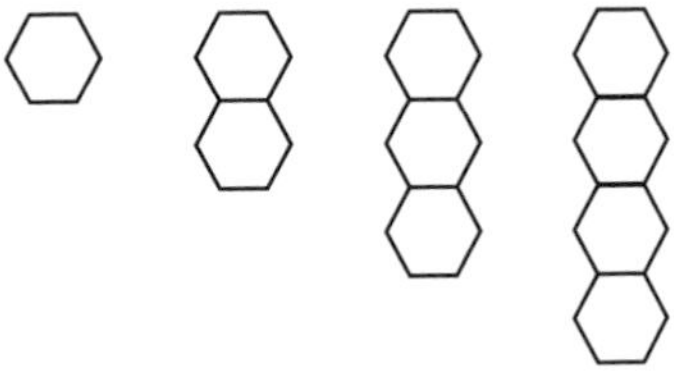

Figure 14 *Tabulating results to help formulate generalizations*

two, three and four hexagons, respectively. The results are tabulated as shown. Pupils then are challenged to predict how many sticks will be needed for chains of five hexagons and six hexagons – and then to check their predictions. This involves recognizing and applying a sequential generalization, such as 'adding 5 each time'. Much more challenging is to predict how many sticks will be needed to construct a chain of, say, 20 hexagons. This involves recognizing and applying a global generalization, such as 'multiply the number of hexagons by 5 and add 1'. More able pupils at the top end of primary schools will be able to express this in algebraic terms: $n = 5m + 1$, where n is the number of sticks needed and m is the number of hexagons. Formulating global generalizations such as these is therefore a key step in the development of algebraic thinking.

FURTHER READING

Chapter 27 of Haylock (2006: 305–22) identifies the making and testing of generalizations as one of twelve key aspects of mathematical reasoning. Haylock discusses the following stages involved in generalizing: conjecturing and checking, using the language of generalization, counterexamples, special cases, hypothesis, explanation and proof. Teachers of younger children are encouraged to read Threlfall's chapter on 'Repeating patterns in the early primary years' (in Orton, 1999). Two other chapters in this excellent book also provide material relevant to this topic: 'Teaching and assessing patterns in number in the primary years' by Frobisher and Threlfall, and 'Pattern in the approach to algebra' by A. Orton and J. Orton.

Deductive and inductive reasoning. Giftedness in mathematics. Investigation (enquiry). Principle learning.

Giftedness in Mathematics

DEFINITION

It is not helpful to attempt to define precisely the concept of giftedness in mathematics. A pragmatic approach (Haylock, 2004: 151) is to use 'gifted in mathematics' to describe the pupil who turns up from time to time in a primary school year group, for whom an intelligent and thoughtful teacher will recognize that the provision in mathematics that is appropriate for the normal range of pupils in that year group is nothing like sufficiently demanding and challenging. Such pupils will be characterized not just by high attainment in conventional mathematics tests of knowledge, skills, understanding and application, but also by higher-order cognitive abilities, such as analysis, synthesis and creativity in mathematical activity.

EXPLANATION AND DISCUSSION

Mathematics is the core subject in the curriculum where exceptional ability can be most marked. Primary school teachers will always have available additional material for their more able pupils in mathematics, to ensure that they are challenged sufficiently and achieve their potential. But sometimes they come across a pupil for whom their normal stock of additional material seems hopelessly inadequate and insufficiently demanding. Such a pupil may be regarded as gifted in mathematics. But what are the key characteristics of giftedness in this subject?

In his model of multiple intelligences, Gardner (2000) identifies a number of distinct kinds of intelligence, which are relatively autonomous and independent of each other. One of these is 'logical-mathematical intelligence', which includes both analysis (systematic and logical reasoning) and synthesis (recognizing patterns and articulating generalizations). These two key strands of mathematical ability reflect the importance of both analytical and synthetic thinking in mathematics. To solve a problem, the mathematician starts by analysing its components, breaking it up into its various parts, determining what is given and what is the goal. Synthesis involves bringing a number of parts together into a whole, for example, when the mathematician formulates a generalization from a number of specific cases.

These two strands are clearly identifiable in various descriptions of the characteristics of pupils with exceptional ability in mathematics (DfEE, 2000: 4; Kennard, 2001: 100; Krutetskii, 1976: 350–1). To summarize these, the following are the ways in which mathematically gifted pupils are usually distinguished from their peers.

- They grasp new material quickly.
- They use mathematical symbols with confidence and move quickly from concrete to abstract.
- They have an inclination to make connections in mathematics.
- They grasp quickly the formal mathematical structure of a problem.
- They generalize patterns and relationships, often unprompted.
- They generalize an approach to solving one problem and recognize when it can be used in other problems.
- They often leave out intermediate steps when solving familiar problems.
- They are prepared to approach problems from different directions and persist in finding solutions.
- They think flexibly and are not constrained by routines and stereotype procedures.
- They provide logical arguments to explain mathematical results.
- They are able to recall generalized results, principles and methods.

Perhaps surprisingly, such lists of the characteristics of mathematically gifted pupils in primary schools do not include prodigious skill in numerical calculations. Krutetskii (1976) found that this was not a necessary component of high mathematical ability. Exceptional ability in mathematics is not just high achievement in the standard elements of the curriculum. For example, all the various accounts of mathematical ability in school children include reference to the importance of cognitive processes such as flexibility, non-rigidity and non-reliance on stereotype procedures, which are key components of creative thinking in mathematics. Creativity in mathematics is therefore a third strand of giftedness in mathematics, to go with analytic and synthetic thinking. Haylock (2004: 159) argues that mathematically gifted pupils are those who are not just high attaining in conventional terms (skills, knowledge, understanding and application) but also highly creative (flexible, divergent, non-rigid and unconventional) in their approach to mathematical tasks.

Because giftedness in mathematics is characterized by higher levels of thinking such as synthesizing solutions, principles and approaches, generating creative approaches to problem solving, thinking analytically and developing logical arguments, then the special needs of these pupils are not met simply by moving them more quickly through the standard curriculum provided for the majority of pupils. To give scope for the development of the specific characteristics of giftedness in mathematics, the following are guidelines for the kinds of experiences needed by mathematically gifted pupils:

- using their mathematical skills and knowledge to solve unfamiliar problems, including opportunities to articulate or determine the problem;
- engaging with problems with too little or too much information;
- learning to clarify the givens and to clarify the goal, and to identify sub-goals in mathematical problem solving;
- having opportunities to explain their reasoning and justify their solutions;
- learning new mathematical content and skills that will open up opportunities for a broader range of experiences of mathematical thinking and processes;
- exploring number patterns arising from geometrical patterns, and vice versa;
- articulating generalizations in words and with algebraic symbols;
- learning to identify independent and dependent variables and to control independent variables systematically;
- using two-way tables for summarizing and exploring patterns in situations with two independent variables;
- having opportunities to investigate, to conjecture, to hypothesize, and to make higher-level generalization;
- having opportunities to identify general principles and to generalize procedures that arise in one situation that can be applied in others;

- being encouraged to persist in problem solving, to try alternative approaches, to call on a wider range of mathematical concepts and facts;
- engaging in tasks that require logical reasoning;
- engaging in tasks where they need to be systematic;
- engaging in tasks where they succeed by being unorthodox, by not adhering to routines, by being flexible, non-rigid, thinking divergently, and adopting original approaches.

PRACTICAL EXAMPLES

One of the authors of this book undertook some research with a group of able pupils in mathematics that included two pupils who exemplify most clearly the difference between high attainment in conventional mathematics and giftedness in this subject.

J: a high attainer, not gifted

J is judged by the class teacher to be a high attainer in mathematics, has a high level of competence in standard learnt routines and does very well in conventional tests. But the researcher found J to be low in confidence and clearly anxious when presented with unfamiliar problems, hiding work from others and reluctant to take risks. J is relatively poor at recognizing number patterns and making generalizations, is slow in making connections in mathematics, and shows rigidity in thinking. Although J may do well in national assessments, at this stage this pupil is not demonstrating the key indicators of being gifted at mathematics.

K: a gifted underachiever

By contrast, K is a very untidy 9-year-old, with poor handwriting skills. K has not been outstanding in normal mathematics classes. The class teacher regards K as an underachiever, careless, not highly motivated and unwilling to work hard.

In one task, the researcher gave K a sheet taken from a newspaper with pages numbered 35, 36, 109, 110. From this K was able quickly to work out how many pages there were in the newspaper. Given the rest of the newspaper K then investigated how the pages were arranged on the sheets. The researcher equipped the pupil with a simple algebraic idea, using n for the number of pages, m for the number of sheets, f for the number of the front page of the four-page folded sheet, b for the back, l and r for the left and right inside pages. K quickly concluded that $n = m \times 4$. The pupil responded to a suggestion to tabulate the numbers of the pages that came together on each sheet of the newspaper:

f	l	r	b
1	2	71	72
3	4	69	70
5	6	67	68
7	8	65	66

and so on …

K was then able to formulate the following generalizations, such as 'l and b are always even', '$l + b = n + 2$' and '$f + r = n$'. K could then explain how the last of these could be used with any one sheet to find the number of pages. The pupil then looked at other newspapers and was able to explain why these generalizations would work in all cases where there were four pages to each sheet. Summarizing K's achievements on a number of tasks, the researcher concluded that this pupil shows many of the qualities of being gifted in mathematics, in particular:

- exceptional ability in grasping the mathematical structure of a problem and in reasoning mathematically;
- ability to articulate generalizations for number patterns, using all four operations and squares of numbers and algebraic notation;
- an appropriate level of self-confidence, persistence and flexibility in tackling unfamiliar problems;
- a memory for new terms for mathematical concepts and ability to use them correctly in new situations.

FURTHER READING

The starting point for any serious study of the nature of giftedness in mathematics must be Krutetskii (1976). Koshy (2000a) provides both theoretical and practical guidance on teaching mathematics to able children. Porter (2005), although not specific to mathematics, provides a rationale for gifted education, as well as comprehensive and practical guidance for working with able children up to about 8 years of age. Also helpful for this age range is the chapter on supporting the gifted child in mathematics in Edwards (1998). A useful resource for teachers is the internet-based material provided by NRICH (www.nrich.maths.org), a project based at the University of Cambridge School of Education, providing curriculum enrichment and learning support in mathematics for very able children of all ages.

RELATED ENTRIES

Creativity in mathematics. Differentiation. Generalization. Problem solving.

Home as a Context for Numeracy

DEFINITION

The pupil's life at home and their life at school are two different contexts in which the skills and concepts of numeracy are developed and applied. Primary teachers should recognize that these two contexts bring with them significantly different sets of numeracy purposes and practices, characterized by the differing values and beliefs of home and school, and the differing norms of social and institutional relations (Street et al., 2005). In this entry, the word 'parent' is used for a responsible adult with whom the child lives.

EXPLANATION AND DISCUSSION

Home is not just a place in which pupils do homework. Primary school teachers should see the pupil's life at home as a meaningful context in which to embed the mathematical knowledge and skills that are to be taught in the curriculum. For example, teachers of young children might use in the classroom a simulation of table-setting at home to develop the concept of one-to-one matching that underpins the child's understanding of number and counting. Or teachers might provide parents with lists of key mathematical vocabulary to reinforce at home in their conversations with children as they travel on the bus, go shopping, have their meals, and so on. Or pupils might be given homework tasks that involve finding around the home some examples of something they are learning about in their mathematics lessons; for example, pupils might be asked to bring in food packaging showing weights in grams up to a kilogram, to add to a class display.

There is clearly value in using the home to support and give meaning to the mathematics being learnt in the classroom. There is also great value in involving parents as much as possible in the child's mathematics education, so that the endeavour is seen as a partnership, with mutual support, shared understanding and a common agenda, as promoted by the IMPACT project (Merttens and Vass, 1993).

However, Street et al. (2005: ch. 2) suggest a more complex analysis of the relationship between home and school in learning mathematics, based on a social approach to the concept of numeracy. They point out that numeracy practices at school and at home differ because they are embedded in different social relations and purposes, and are characterized by differing values and beliefs. At school, for example, the teacher has control of what will be learnt, how it will be learnt, and what counts as the best way of doing a mathematical task. Mathematical activity is carried out for an educational purpose defined by the teacher, to meet the demands of the school curriculum and national assessments. At home, by contrast, numeracy practices are determined by domestic purposes and the child has a level of involvement or control over how and why their mathematical knowledge is used and their choice of mathematical processes.

This analysis presents a challenge for teachers: not to look on the home just as a context for the mathematics the child is learning at school, but also to embrace those numeracy processes that occur in the normal course of events within the home context. This will require giving time for pupils to talk about and share activities they engage in at home which constitute any form of mathematical activity, and to show that the purposes and processes used are valued and as valid as those undertaken at school. Street et al. (2005: ch. 7) show that the degree of consonance or dissonance between numeracy practice at school and that provided by the cultural context of the child's home can explain different achievements in numeracy; so it is important that teachers seek as far as possible to understand what the child brings with them from home and to work with this, rather than against it.

PRACTICAL EXAMPLES

To illustrate the range of ways in which teachers might make use of the pupils' home as a context for learning mathematics, here are four examples on the theme of handling money in shopping transactions.

1. For homework the pupils take home a worksheet with examples of making purchases and calculating the change from £1, £5 or £10, to reinforce what they have been learning at school that week. This approach is the least imaginative use of the home for homework, which does little to motivate pupils and often causes unnecessary conflict between children and parents; but it presumably has some value in communicating to interested parents what their child is being taught in mathematics lessons.

2. Pupils are required to ask a parent to help them to identify six things at home that cost up to £10, to work out the change from £1, £5 or £10, as appropriate, and to bring this information into school the next day, to be used as examples in a class discussion.

3. Pupils are asked to write a simple diary for a week of all the transactions involving money with which they are involved outside the classroom. Parents are sent a letter requesting that they support their child in this and that the child be allowed to bring the diary into school. The teacher (sensitively) uses extracts from various diaries as starting points for teaching purposes.

4. At a parents' evening the teacher invites parents to share the experiences that their children have of shopping, how their children obtain and use their own money and how they make purchases. This is done to raise the teacher's awareness of the numeracy practices that exist in the child's life outside school, so that these can be built upon in the classroom. The emphasis here has shifted away from the school telling parents how mathematics should be done, to parents telling teachers how it is actually done in their own cultural and social settings.

FURTHER READING

Merrtens (in Thompson, 1999), in a chapter entitled 'Family numeracy', explores the involvement of parents in their children's learning of mathematics and the thorny question of homework. Street et al. (2005) provide some revealing case studies that show how achievement in mathematics is affected by: significant differences between home and school numeracy practices; aspects of communication between home and school; areas of conflict between home and school; and differences in resources and funds of knowledge in homes and schools. There are two helpful chapters in Carruthers and Worthington (2006): 'Bridging the gap between home and school mathematics', and 'Involving parents and families'.

RELATED ENTRIES

Cross-cultural mathematics. Meaningful context. Numeracy.

Informal Calculation Method

DEFINITION

An informal calculation method is any way of doing a numerical calculation by written or mental methods, or a combination of these, without using a standard algorithm. A characteristic of a successful informal method is that the method chosen will often be determined by the actual numbers involved in the calculation, and not just by the operation required (addition, subtraction, multiplication or division). Another characteristic is that the method will draw on and be determined by existing knowledge of numerical facts and relationships.

EXPLANATION AND DISCUSSION

Consider, for example, 25 × 24. An 11-year-old in a primary school might be able to use a standard multiplication algorithm to calculate the result here (such as 'long multiplication'), but the numbers involved might suggest that an informal method would be more appropriate and simpler. If the pupil's existing number knowledge includes awareness that 25 multiplied by 4 is 100, then whenever 25 turns up in a multiplication the pupil might be on the lookout for an opportunity to multiply it by 4. This might lead to spotting a potentially useful relationship between 4 and 24 (4 is a factor of 24). So the pupil might deal with the calculation informally as follows:

$$
\begin{aligned}
25 \times 24 &= 25 \times (4 \times 6) \\
&= (25 \times 4) \times 6 \\
&= 100 \times 6 \\
&= 600.
\end{aligned}
$$

Haylock (2006: 22) has coined the term 'adhocorithm' for this type of informal, non-standard process, to contrast it with an algorithm – which is a step-by-step method for a calculation that is applied more or less regardless of the numbers involved and any relationships between them. An argument for encouraging the use of these adhocorithms is that, because they are based on relationships between numbers, they are more likely to involve reasoning with understanding than to rely on rote learning of recipes and procedures.

The QCA report on the 1997 national mathematics tests for 11-year-olds in England noted that many pupils showed a preference for such informal methods, even though at the time these were rarely taught specifically in primary classrooms. An example is one pupil's written account of a problem that required the subtraction of 82p from £5:

From 82p to 90 is eight, from 90 [to] 1 pound is 10, add them together with the other pounds. £4.18. (QCA, 1997: 19)

Prior to the introduction of the National Numeracy Strategy in English primary schools (DfEE, 1999b), this kind of approach was often regarded by primary school teachers as in some way inferior to the standard taught procedures, and not as valid as the 'proper' way, such as using the decomposition method for subtraction. Consequently, such methods were often not taught specifically and certainly not encouraged. Analysis of children's answers in the national tests, however, indicated that in more demanding questions children tended to show a greater incidence of invented strategies, as they 'thought their way into the mathematics' (QCA, 1997: 18). In multiplication and division calculations, 11-year-olds attempting to apply a standard algorithm often went astray. More successful were those who used non-standard approaches, such as this pupil's calculation of 24 multiplied by 12:

> 288, because I know the sum 12×12 and [this] equals 144, and I just doubled it. (QCA, 1997: 20)

This is a good example of how an individual can draw on their existing number knowledge and the relationships between the numbers in the calculation to formulate an effective, ad hoc, informal method.

Findings such as these were the background to the recognition in the Numeracy Strategy of the value and validity of children's informal methods in learning mathematics in primary schools. Publications written to support the Numeracy Strategy (QCA, 1999a, 1999b) advocate teaching approaches that encourage pupils to develop confidence with informal methods before they are taught the standard algorithms, and to continue using them, except when the numbers in the calculations are such that the standard algorithm is the simplest and most efficient method. However, in their studies of the early stages of children learning to handle number, Carruthers and Worthington (2006) argue that personal methods of young children continue to be insufficiently valued by teachers and their informal jottings are not recognized as useful aids to calculation. Although informal jottings are recommended in official documents, teachers appear to be unsure about how to promote them, preferring instead to impose a formal structure on children's written mathematics through worksheets.

PRACTICAL EXAMPLES

The strategies used in the examples above are typical of informal approaches that can be taught specifically to primary school pupils: doing subtractions (such as £5 – 82p) by ad hoc additions to get from the smaller number to the larger; and relating a calculation to a known number fact (such as relating 24×12 to 12×12). There is space here to mention just three further examples of the key strategies that pupils in primary schools might be taught to support them in gaining confidence in developing and using informal methods of calculation.

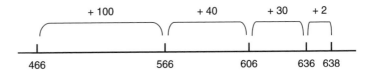

Figure 15 *466 + 172 calculated on an empty number line*

The empty number line

In the primary school classroom, use of the so-called 'empty number line' is an effective way of modelling for pupils a range of informal methods of addition and subtraction calculations. One example of addition is shown in Figure 15, for the calculation of 172 + 466. The calculation is done by breaking up the 172 into 100 + 40 + 30 + 2 and adding these bit by bit to the 466. The approach here uses a number of key strategies that could be taught specifically to pupils and which are characteristic of informal methods of addition:

- starting with the bigger number and adding on the smaller number;
- using a 'front-end' approach, that is, starting by adding on the hundreds rather than the units, as in the standard addition algorithm;
- partitioning, that is, breaking up the 172 into a number of parts;
- bridging across the 100s, by choosing to break the 70 in 172 into 40 + 30, to help the adding-on process as it passes through 600.

Use of doubling in multiplication

Pupils can be taught to deal informally with many multiplication calculations by using previously developed skills in doubling. An efficient way of dealing with the multiplication 28 × 18, for example, would be by repeatedly doubling the 28, as follows:

$$28 \times 2 = 56$$
$$28 \times 4 = 112$$
$$28 \times 8 = 224$$
$$28 \times 16 = 448.$$

Hence, because 18 = 16 + 2, 28 × 18 = 448 + 56 = 504.

Division by ad hoc addition

Primary pupils can do division calculations by an informal method that is based on ad hoc addition. For example, to calculate 306 ÷ 18, a pupil

```
10 | 180
 5 |  90
   | 270
 1 |  18
   | 288
 1 |  18
17 | 306
```

Figure 16 *Informal calculation of 306 ÷ 18*

might start with 10 eighteens (180), then add on 5 eighteens (90), to get 270, then add on another eighteen to get 288, and one more eighteen to get to 306. Adding up the number of eighteens used to reach the target, 306 ÷ 18 is equal to 10 + 5 + 1 + 1 = 17. The calculation might be laid out as shown in Figure 16. The number of steps that would be used in an approach like this would be dependent on the confidence of the pupil with the numbers involved.

FURTHER READING

Two helpful booklets (QCA, 1999a, 1999b), on mental calculation strategies and written calculations, were written to support the implementation of the Numeracy Strategy in England. For a fascinating study comparing the informal calculation procedures used by young vendors on the streets of Recife in Brazil with the formal methods taught in schools, have a look at Nunes et al. (1993). Carruthers and Worthington (2006) provide significant insights into the creative ways in which young children use informal jottings and personal methods. Ambrose et al. provide an analysis of research into children's informal multiplication and division methods, in a chapter entitled 'Children's invention of multidigit multiplication and division algorithms' (in Baroody and Dowker, 2003).

RELATED ENTRIES

Algorithm. Mental calculation.

DEFINITION

Investigation (or enquiry) in mathematics is understood in this entry to refer to a task given to pupils that uses mathematics and which to varying degrees gives the pupils the opportunity to pose their own questions, to determine their own approaches, to make their own discoveries, and to articulate and communicate their findings to others.

EXPLANATION AND DISCUSSION

Mathematical investigation achieved particular prominence in school mathematics in the UK following the publication of the influential report of the Cockcroft Enquiry (Cockcroft, 1982). In its famous paragraph 243, the report listed six components that should be present in mathematics teaching at all levels: exposition by the teacher; discussion between teachers and pupils and between pupils themselves; appropriate practical work; consolidation and practice; problem solving; and investigational work. However, in giving such prominence to problem solving and investigational work, Cockcroft was doing no more than lending support to what was emerging in the 1970s and 1980s as good practice in mathematics teaching. This was characterized by less of an emphasis on didactic teaching of routine processes and more of an emphasis on encouraging pupils to pose questions, to conjecture and to engage actively in developing strategies for solving problems. Following the Cockcroft Report there was a flurry of activity and publications promoting the incorporation of investigations in the mathematics curriculum, both primary and secondary.

The introduction of the Numeracy Strategy framework (DfEE, 1999b) brought about a decline in the use of investigative approaches in primary mathematics classrooms in England. This was partly because the framework's yearly teaching programmes, which were adopted by many schools, left no scope for extended activities or anything other than focusing on specific objectives in terms of knowledge and skills. However, the review in 2006 of the National Strategy for primary schools has clearly once again embedded investigational work (now called 'enquiry') in the primary school mathematics curriculum. Enquiry features as one of the five key themes within the *Using and Applying Mathematics* strand in the revised framework for primary school mathematics. The guidelines provided for this strand provide a positive slant on the experience of primary pupils involved in investigative mathematics: 'Learners are engaged by successful and exciting learning. They become involved in finding out for themselves, asking and answering questions, and sharing what they have discovered with others' (DfES, 2006b: 9).

Building on this description, we would suggest that the key components of successful mathematical investigations are that they provide opportunities for pupils to:

- engage with a task they find challenging, interesting, stimulating;
- pose their own questions about mathematical situations;
- plan their own approaches;
- use important mathematical skills and knowledge they have learnt already;
- make their own discoveries and experience the satisfaction of finding things out for themselves;
- articulate and communicate what they have found out to others;
- add to their developing understanding of mathematical concepts and relationships.

The DfES guidelines suggest that initially children will be given the questions to investigate by their teachers, but 'as they get more skilled at planning and organizing their strategies and thoughts, and more confident at sustaining such activity, new questions will arise. These can be gathered, discussed and refined, so that children can pursue those that appeal to them' (DfES, 2006b: 9).

The importance of using investigations in mathematics in primary schools is not just that they are enjoyable experiences, which will motivate pupils to engage with mathematics and which are likely to promote positive attitudes to the subject. Nor is it just that learning makes more impact on us when we have discovered something for ourselves. It is also that when engaged in investigations learners will have to go beyond just rote learning – relying on the use and application of algorithms, rules and routine procedures – to develop their own understanding of general relationships. Jaworski (2003: 2) argues that 'inquiry or investigative methods in mathematics teaching are seen to fit with a constructivist view of knowledge and learning as they offer challenges to stimulate mathematical thinking and create opportunities for critical reflection on mathematical understanding'. To ensure that the experience of engaging in an investigation is worthwhile, it is essential therefore that teachers spend time with pupils after they have completed their enquiries, helping them to reflect on what they have discovered and to recognize what of all that they have been doing is significant and how it relates to other things they have previously learnt or experienced.

PRACTICAL EXAMPLES

Here are five examples of starting points for investigation by pupils at various stages in primary school. To varying degrees, each of these examples provides opportunities for pupils to frame their own questions, to determine their own approaches, and to make and articulate their own discoveries.

1. What things in the classroom can you find that are heavier than a pencil and lighter than a pair of scissors? Make up some other questions like this to investigate.
2. You have a box of sticks of different lengths: 4 cm, 6 cm, 8 cm, 10 cm and 12 cm. Close your eyes and pick up three sticks. Use them to form the three sides of a triangle. If you can …
3. Here's an interesting situation to explore! Meg and her father have the same birthday. This year it just happens that Meg's age is her father's age with the digits reversed. Meg wonders if this will ever happen again … or if it has ever happened before …
4. You have four sheets of paper of different sizes: A2, A3, A4 and A5. Find out as many interesting things as you can about these paper sizes and how they are related. What would you expect to find if you were given a sheet of A1 paper? Or A0 paper? Or A6 paper? Can you find any pieces of card or paper at school or at home that are A7 or A10? How would you know?
5. Figure 17 shows what happens when you write the sequence of numbers 5, 4, 3, 2, 1, over and over again in a grid with four squares in each row. Using squared paper, continue this for ten more rows. Then write down any interesting patterns that you notice in the ways the numbers are arranged. Investigate whether these patterns

5	4	3	2
1	5	4	3
2	1	5	4
3	2	1	5
4	3	2	1
5	4	3	2
1			

Figure 17 *What patterns do you notice?*

or other patterns occur for other sequences of numbers (such as 6, 5, 4, 3, 2, 1). Then, what about other numbers of squares in the rows of the grid? Can you explain why these patterns happen?

FURTHER READING

Burton (1984) provides a lively, challenging but practical guide to problem solving and investigational work in mathematics, with analysis of a number of examples of pupils engaging with mathematical enquiry. For a useful source of ideas for investigations see Thyer (1993). For those working with younger children, the approach advocated by Tucker (2005) incorporates many of the principles and features of investigative work described above. A key document in relation to mathematical enquiry is the guidance *Using and Applying Mathematics* in the National Strategy for primary schools in England (DfES, 2006b).

RELATED ENTRIES

Constructivism. Generalization. Problem solving. Using and applying mathematics.

Language Difficulties
in Mathematics

DEFINITION

The particular language difficulties inherent in mathematics that are discussed in this entry relate to vocabulary, syntax, abstract and natural language, miscues in word problems, and the predominance of structure over content.

EXPLANATION AND DISCUSSION

The importance of language in learning mathematics cannot be overstated. We understand mathematical ideas by making connections between language, symbols, pictures and real-life situations (Haylock and Cockburn, 2003: 1–19). Mathematical concepts to be understood and used have to be associated with a word or a phrase. In a summary of research into the development of mathematical ideas in young children, Perry and Dockett (2002: 101) conclude that 'without sufficient language to communicate the ideas being developed, children will be at a loss to interact with their peers and their teachers and therefore will have their mathematical development seriously curtailed'. Because of the significance of language in learning mathematics, it is important that teachers are aware of the particular difficulties and complexities of the way language is used in this subject. Five categories of these are discussed below.

Vocabulary

The difficulties associated with the technical vocabulary of mathematics include the following.

1. Mathematics uses a number of technical words that are not usually met or used by primary school pupils outside mathematics lessons. Examples might include 'parallelogram' and 'multiplication'. Such words are not being reinforced in everyday usage and are therefore

not being given greater meaning through employment in a range of contexts. The existence of a discrete set of mathematical terminology also encourages pupils to perceive mathematics as being something that happens in school that is unrelated to their everyday lives outside school.

2. There are words that are used in everyday English, which have different or much more specific meanings in mathematics. For example, in relation to subtraction the 'difference between 8 and 13' is not that one has one digit and the other has two digits. Other familiar examples would include: 'volume' (in everyday English used mainly for levels of sound); and 'right' as used in 'right angle' (not the opposite of a left angle!). Mathematics uses 'odd' to refer to every other counting number, which is hardly consistent with the everyday use of the word (see Pimm, 1987: 89). Clearly, primary school teachers have to anticipate possible confusions when using such words as these.

3. Words in mathematics are characteristically used with precise meanings. But in ordinary everyday English, many mathematical words are misused or used with a degree of sloppiness, which can be a barrier to pupils' understanding of mathematical concepts. 'Sugar cubes' are usually cuboids, but not all of them are actually cubes. Adults do not mean a time interval of one second when they say, 'Just a second!' The phrase 'a fraction of the cost' uses the word 'fraction' imprecisely to mean 'a small part of'. And the word 'half' is often used to mean one of two parts not necessarily equal. Moreover, many teachers themselves use mathematical language carelessly, such as confusing 'amount' with 'number', or using 'sum' to refer to a calculation other than an addition.

Syntax

We provide here two examples of the difficulties of syntax that occur frequently for pupils trying to make sense of mathematical statements.

1. The first difficulty relates to the subtle uses of prepositions in a number of the basic statements we make in mathematics. Consider, for example, the differences in meaning between: (a) 'divide 25 by 10' and 'divide 25 into 10'; (b) 'reduce this price by £20' and 'reduce this price to £20'; (c) 'share twelve between three' and 'share twelve with three'. Teachers also need to be aware of ambiguities associated with

prepositions in some mathematical statements, such as: 'what is 10 divided into 5?' (2 or 0.5?); and 'how much is 5 more than 3?' (2 or 8?).

2. Teachers should also recognize the syntactical complexity of many of the statements they make and the questions they pose in mathematics. Consider, for example, this question: 'Which number between 25 and 30 cannot be divided equally by either 2 or 3?' To grasp this, the pupil not only has to hold in their mind a number of pieces of detailed information, but also has to relate these together in the precise way implied by the complex syntax of the sentence. It is a hugely demanding task, but not untypical of what is demanded of primary school pupils doing mathematics.

ABSTRACT AND NATURAL LANGUAGE

Pupils need to learn correct, formal mathematical language. So, for example, the collection of symbols '37 − 14 = 23' is read formally as 'thirty-seven subtract fourteen equals twenty-three'. This is a purely abstract statement, dealing with concepts expressed in abstract language. However, if these symbols were a model of some real-life situation there would also be the natural language that describes the situation, such as: 'If I have 37p and I spend 14p, then I have 23p left.' Giving time to establishing the connections between the formal abstract language that goes with the symbols and the natural language that describes the concrete situations modelled by the symbols is a major part of the agenda for primary teachers of mathematics. Boero et al. (2002: 243), in a review of research in this area, stress the importance of natural language as 'a mediator between mental processes, specific symbolic expressions, and logical organizations in mathematical activities'. However, a major difficulty is that pupils have to learn to connect the same formal, abstract language and the associated symbols with the natural language associated with a range of very different real-life situations. So, the same symbols used above could be associated with the language of taking away, or making comparisons, or finding how much more is needed, and so on, in a range of contexts, such as sets of objects, money, length, time, mass and capacity (Haylock and Cockburn, 2003: 46–58).

Miscues in word problems

One of the major language difficulties in mathematics is the way in which pupils will sometimes respond incorrectly to verbal cues in word problems. For example, in a word problem that requires a subtraction but which contains the word 'more', the word 'more', because it is naturally associated with addition, will act as a miscue and prompt pupils to add the numbers in the problem. For example, 25 would be a common answer given by 8-year-olds to this question: 'John has now collected 18 tokens. That's 7 more than he had last week. How many tokens did he have last week?'

The predominance of structure over content

'Meg has saved up £18.80 towards buying the complete *The Lord of the Rings* DVD set, which costs £26.50. How much more does she need?' To some primary school pupils, the most intriguing aspects of this question are likely to be in the narrative content (Pimm, 1987: 12–14), promoting responses such as, 'She could get them cheaper in .... '. But in a mathematics context, the content has to be disregarded in favour of the underlying structure, from which must emerge the subtraction calculation, 26.50 – 18.80. The structure of the sentence has to be predominant over the narrative content. This rather artificial way of responding to language is a distinctive requirement in dealing with word problems in mathematics. But then, when it comes to interpreting the result of the calculation (such as the 7.7 obtained when 26.50 – 18.80 is entered on a calculator) recognition of the original narrative content of the problem becomes essential again.

PRACTICAL EXAMPLES

Two practical suggestions for focusing on mathematical language are given below.

Stories for calculations

One of the best ways of gaining insights into children's understanding of mathematical ideas is to analyse their use of natural language to write stories for calculations written in symbols. For example, given the division $12 \div 3$, one pupil wrote: 'Tim had 12 cakes he shared them out with 3 of his friends' (Haylock and Cockburn, 2003: 79). The use of the preposition 'with' here reveals a misunderstanding of the notion of sharing in the context of division. Another pupil wrote this story for the subtraction, $12 - 3$: 'There were 12 soldiers, 3 were ill, how many were not ill?' (Haylock and Cockburn, 2003: 48). This use of the word 'not' reveals a good understanding of the connection between subtraction and the complement of a set.

Language patterns

Because of the syntactical complexity of many mathematical statements primary school teachers should spend time helping pupils to master significant language patterns, particularly those involving subtle uses of prepositions. For example, a key language pattern associated with division is used here: '24 shared equally between six is four each.' Special emphasis should be placed on the patterns of statements using the language of comparison (Haylock and Cockburn, 2003: 50–2), which are particularly complex for many pupils. For example, the structure of the statement '12 is 3 more than 9' would be encountered in a number of contexts such as:

- the £12 CD costs £3 more than the £9 CD;
- the 12 kg box is 3 kg heavier than the 9 kg box;
- the 12 cm strip is 3 cm longer than the 9 cm strip.

These statements should always be accompanied by the equivalent language patterns using the lesser quantity as the subject:

- the £9 CD costs £3 less than the £12 CD;
- the 9 kg box is 3 kg lighter than the 12 kg box;
- the 9 cm strip is 3 cm shorter than the 12 cm strip.

FURTHER READING

Wigley's chapter, 'Approaching number through language' (in Thompson, 1997), deals with some of the language aspects of young children learning to count. A key text on language in mathematics is Pimm (1987). Verschaffel and De Corte provide a comprehensive review and discussion of children's responses to arithmetic word problems (chapter 4, in Nunes and Bryant, 1997). Those interested in how to help pupils whose poor language skills impinge on their learning of mathematics should refer to Grauberg (1998).

Concept learning. Making connections. Modelling process (representing). Talk.

Low Attainment

DEFINITION

Low attainment is used here to refer to the achievement of a pupil in primary school that falls some way below the majority of pupils in the year group or the level expected of average pupils. The term is used loosely, so 'low attainers' might be, for example, those pupils in a small bottom set in a year group where pupils are put into three or more sets for mathematics lessons, or the least successful four or five pupils in a mixed-ability class with a typical range of achievement in mathematics.

EXPLANATION AND DISCUSSION

This entry is not therefore just about pupils in primary schools who have been identified as having special educational needs, which may or may not have significant implications for their attainment in mathematics. It is more generally about what Dowker (2004), in a review of research, refers to as 'children with mathematical difficulties'. Dowker (2004: 4) suggests, for example, that 'within the British educational system … children who are working at level 1 at age 7, or level 3 at age 11, have some degree of mathematical difficulty'. (The expected National Curriculum levels for these ages are levels 2 and 4 respectively.)

Low attainment in mathematics is not a unidimensional phenomenon. It can have a number of different characteristics, can present itself in many different forms and can be associated with a complex range of factors. Many of the pupils who are low attainers in mathematics are

low attainment

105

low attainers in most areas of the curriculum. Haylock (1986) found that teachers reported this to be definitely or probably true for 79 per cent of a sample of 215 mathematically low-attaining pupils aged 10 to 11 years. But some pupils whose attainment is generally average or above average across the curriculum have particular difficulties in mathematics. And Dowker (2004: 2) reports that 'some have specific delays in arithmetic, which will eventually be resolved; and some have persisting, specific problems in arithmetic'.

The term 'dyscalculia' is sometimes used to refer to the mathematical equivalent of dyslexia or dyspraxia. It refers to a neurological dysfunction shown by a very specific inability to process numerical information, unlike anything that might be observed in the normal range of pupils. Dyscalculia may be developmental or sometimes caused by brain damage; it should be regarded as an exceptional condition requiring specialist help. It is not a term that should be applied to all pupils who have difficulties in number work.

Factors associated with low attainment often include reading and other language problems, perceptual difficulties, such as reversals of figures or poor spatial discrimination, social and emotional problems that show themselves in poor behaviour in school, and mathematics anxiety (Haylock, 1991: 41–4). Other contributing factors might include those that would affect a pupil's learning across the curriculum: poor motor skills, frequent absences, a difficult home situation, physical disabilities, poor health, alienation from school generally and difficulty in concentrating.

Houssart (2004) found some pupils in the lowest mathematics sets in primary schools to have difficulties in some specific aspects of mathematics. For example, some pupils are more comfortable with routine written algorithms and others with mental calculation. Houssart's research (2004: 165) revealed a marked inconsistency in the performance of low-attaining pupils in mathematics. This could sometimes be explained by the way the task was presented, or by factors outside school affecting the mood of the pupil, but not always.

Houssart's observations led also to the conclusion that low-attaining children can sometimes surprise their teachers with what they can do. Haylock (1991: 66–7) provides examples of the 'unexpected competence and commitment' that can be shown by some low attainers when the mathematical task catches their imagination and concludes: 'Time and time again low-attaining pupils surprise their teachers with what they can do when they are given purposeful tasks, real problems, and the opportunity to use mathematics to make things happen.' De Geest et al. (2002) report evidence that low attainers can exhibit qualities of mathematical thinking characteristic of high attainers, if the material is presented in particular ways appropriate to the individuals. For example, with the right kind of tasks, low attainers have shown the ability to use examples and counter-examples, to generalize, to develop efficient methods of working and to move to higher levels of abstraction (Harries, 2001; Watson, 2000).

Dowker (2004: 2) cites 'inadequate or inappropriate teaching' as a contributing factor in low attainment. Haylock (1991: 44–50) argues that, in terms of meeting the needs of low-attaining pupils, the most significant shortcomings in teaching include: an inflexible use of a commercially produced mathematics scheme; moving pupils on too quickly to new processes before they have really mastered the prerequisite material; teaching mathematical processes as meaningless routines; and giving pupils too many disembedded tasks with neither meaningful context nor purpose. De Geest et al. (2002) suggest that teachers who work successfully with low-attaining pupils in mathematics are those who let their students construct their own meaning and make sense of mathematics, give them time to think and to complete tasks, develop mathematical tasks from pupils' own questions, and provide an emotionally secure environment.

PRACTICAL EXAMPLES

Primary school teachers concerned about meeting the needs of the lowest-attaining pupils in their classes, should recognize that there will not be one approach that suits all such pupils, because the factors contributing to their low attainment will be complex and varied. However, the consensus of opinion of those who have researched low attainment in mathematics would seem to support at least the following ten approaches to teaching and learning as being relevant to the majority of such pupils.

- Give particular attention and time within mathematics lessons to the development of language in mathematics.
- Do not rely on the written word (textbooks, worksheets, and so on) as the major means of communicating instructions.
- Be prepared to try several different kinds of mathematical activity in searching for those that will catch the interest and commitment of different pupils.

- Set mathematical activities in contexts that are meaningful for pupils.
- Make as much use as possible of mathematical activities that are purposeful from the perspective of the pupil.
- Expect practical tasks and real-life problem solving to be more likely to motivate low-attaining pupils than abstract mathematical investigations.
- Diagnose particular difficulties in understanding and mastery of skills and provide material focused on remedying these difficulties.
- Use small steps in setting short-term targets for pupils' learning, making these clear to pupils and rewarding every little success.
- Allow pupils to build on approaches to calculation that make most sense to them.
- Allow freer access to calculators to enable pupils who have difficulties with calculations to focus on the mathematics involved in practical or problem-solving tasks, rather than just the calculations.

FURTHER READING

Two books quoted above (Haylock, 1991; Houssart, 2004), both rooted in classroom experience with low-attaining pupils, can be recommended for further reading. Dowker (2004) provides an analysis of what research reveals about the nature of mathematical difficulties experienced by pupils in primary schools and the effectiveness of various approaches to intervention. Those interested in dyscalculia might look at Henderson et al. (2003), or *Guidance to Support Pupils with Dyslexia and Dyscalculia* (DfES, 2001). The DfES (2005) has produced a pack of materials, *Supporting Children with Gaps in their Mathematical Understanding*, which target a number of very specific difficulties in number. A recommendation for those who teach younger children is chapter 18 on supporting low attainers in mathematics in Edwards (1998).

RELATED ENTRIES

Language difficulties in mathematics. Meaningful context. Purposeful activity.

Making Connections

DEFINITION

Making connections in mathematics refers to the process in learning whereby the pupil constructs understanding of mathematical ideas through a growing awareness of relationships between concrete experiences, language, pictures and mathematical symbols. Understanding and mastery of mathematical material develops through the learner's organization of these relationships into networks of connections.

EXPLANATION AND DISCUSSION

Haylock and Cockburn (2003: 3–8) offer the model illustrated in Figure 18 as a simple way of discussing how children's understanding can be developed, particularly in relation to their understanding of number and arithmetic operations.

The model is based on the idea that the development of understanding involves making cognitive connections between some new material or some new experience and our existing ideas. If we cannot make connections then we have to resort to trying to learn by rote. The more connected are our experiences, the more secure and the more useful is the learning. Our understanding of complex mathematical concepts, such as subtraction, equality or place value, for example, can be conceived of as a process of gradually constructing networks of connections. This notion can be perceived in some form or other in most theoretical models of learning mathematics. Piaget, for example, described the development of understanding in terms of the learner relating new experiences to their existing cognitive structures, by assimilation and accommodation, to develop what he called 'schemas' (Piaget, 1953).

When children are involved in number work there are four kinds of things that they engage with:

- real, physical objects (concrete experience), such as counters, toys, containers, fingers, dice, groups of children, board games, sticks and stones, and so on;

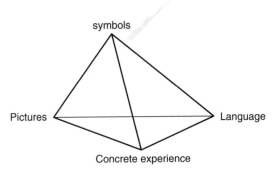

symbols

Pictures

Language

Concrete experience

Figure 18 *Making connections*

- language – both formal, abstract mathematical language (such as 'subtract' and 'equals') and natural language that describes an experience (such as 'take away' and 'how many are left?');
- pictures, particularly sorting and matching diagrams, number strips and number lines, pictograms, and simple block diagrams and bar charts;
- mathematical symbols, particularly those used for numbers (0, 1, 2, ...), operations (+, –, ×, ÷) and equality (=).

These are the building blocks of experiences with which pupils in primary schools construct their mathematical understanding. Liebeck (1990) proposes that children's understanding involves building up connections between these four components through sequential experience, starting with concrete experiences, then adding in the appropriate language, and then pictures and finally the mathematical symbols. Haylock and Cockburn (2003) do not see the model as implying a fixed sequence, but are more concerned to raise teachers' awareness of the need to provide experiences that help to establish such connections as the basis for developing children's understanding.

PRACTICAL EXAMPLES

Children's understanding of subtraction illustrates powerfully the model of making connections. There is a wide range of concrete experiences and associated natural language that have to be connected with the formal language of 'subtract' and the mathematical symbol for subtraction (–). For example, 'twelve subtract nine equals three' (in symbols, 12 – 9 = 3) can be connected with:

- counting out 12 cubes, taking away 9 and counting how many are left;
- having 12p to spend in the class shop, but spending only 9p and having 3p left to spend;
- matching a set of 12 ducks and a set of 9 chickens in the model farm and finding that there are 3 more ducks or 3 fewer chickens;
- having 9 plastic eggs in a box that holds 12, and finding that 3 more are needed to fill the box;
- counting the 9 children in a group of 12 that walked to school today and noting that there were 3 children who did not walk to school;
- comparing a rod of 12 linked red cubes with a rod of 9 blue ones, to find the difference, how many more red, or how many fewer blue;
- comparing a stick 12 cm in length with one of 9 cm in length, to find out how much shorter or longer is one than the other;
- placing 12 red counters in one pan of a balance and 9 blue in the other and then finding how many more blue are needed to balance the red.

This list, which is far from exhaustive, illustrates what a complex network of connections there is to be established. Then Figure 19 illustrates some of the pictures associated with this subtraction that pupils must also learn to connect with the language and symbols, to further their understanding. These include:

- by counting off 9, partitioning a set of 12 into subsets of 9 and 3;
- comparing two sets, one of 9 and one of 12, by matching, to determine how many more in one set or how many fewer in the other;
- a subset of 9 within a set of 12, with 3 that are not in the subset;
- comparing columns of 9 and 12 in a block graph;

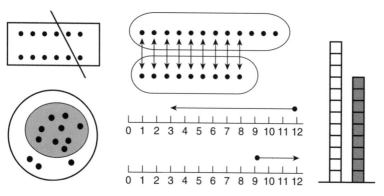

Figure 19 *Pictures to be connected with the subtraction, 12 – 9 = 3*

- counting back 9 steps starting at 12 on a number line;
- counting on from 9 to 12 on a number line.

The importance of having such a network of connections in place is illustrated by the difficulties many pupils will have later on in understanding a subtraction involving a negative number, such as '5 – (–3)'. This cannot be understood if subtraction is connected only with the language and experience of taking away and finding how many are left or how much is left. However, a pupil whose understanding of a subtraction like '12 – 9 = 3' includes connecting it with counting on from 9 to 12 on a number line can readily assimilate the experience of counting on from –3 to 5, and hence can understand that $5 - (-3) = 8$.

FURTHER READING

Liebeck's *How Children Learn Mathematics* (1990) is very readable and well worth reading. The model of learning based on the idea of making connections outlined above is explained in more detail in chapter 1 of Haylock and Cockburn (2003); this is then used as the theoretical framework throughout the book for consideration of the number curriculum for children aged 3 to 8 years. Turner and McCullogh (2004) emphasize teaching strategies that seek to establish relationships between language, symbolic notation and pictorial representation.

RELATED ENTRIES

Concept learning. Constructivism. Meaningful learning. Rote learning.

Match and Mismatch

DEFINITION

The concept of match and mismatch in this entry refers to the extent to which the tasks that pupils are given to do in mathematics in primary schools match or fail to match their individual competences.

EXPLANATION AND DISCUSSION

Match and mismatch are neglected concepts in contemporary writing about teaching mathematics, reflected in the fact that the words do not appear in the indexes of most of the currently published books about teaching primary mathematics. But they are key ideas, which are important in relation to differentiation and which repay detailed analysis and awareness on the part of the teacher.

The aim of good matching is to 'avoid the twin pitfalls of demanding too much and expecting too little' (Bennett et al., 1984: 41). In their study of the quality of the learning experiences of pupils aged 6 to 8 years, Bennett's team found that a significant proportion of the work given to pupils in mathematics was not well matched to the pupils' current attainment. This study provides a helpful framework for discussion of match and mismatch in mathematics. Teachers have a number of different kinds of purposes in planning tasks for pupils, including practice, incremental learning, and enrichment. Bennett's research team identified what would count as mismatch within each of these categories.

Practice

The demand made on the pupil in practice tasks is to increase the fluency or speed of performance, for example, in completing a worksheet of additions of 2-digit numbers, having previously been taught and learnt the skills involved. The task does not match the pupil's competences if the pupil has not previously mastered the skills being practised and continues to make a number of errors or struggles to complete the task. In this case the mismatch is an overestimation of the child's competence. Mismatch can also occur if the practice task does not actually increase the pupil's fluency or speed. In this case the mismatch is an underestimation of the child's competence and the practice task is a waste of their time.

Incremental learning

In an incremental learning task the teacher's expectation is that the task will promote learning by taking the pupil forward a small step from their existing understanding and mastery of skills. For example, having learnt how to use compensation to add mentally numbers ending in 9 (such as adding 29 by adding 30 and subtracting 1), an incremental learning task would involve using this process to add numbers ending in 8 (such as adding 28 by adding 30 and subtracting 2). Mismatch (underestimation) in incremental learning tasks occurs when it transpires that the pupil can complete the tasks with a high level of fluency and accuracy, and could even apply the same principle to the next task in the sequence (such as adding 27 by adding 30 and subtracting 3, or adding 290 by adding 300 and subtracting 10). Mismatch (overestimation) is shown when the child struggles with the task and makes numerous errors or clearly fails to understand, suggesting that they had not really understood or mastered the previous work on which this task is built.

Enrichment

The demand made on the pupil in an enrichment task is that recently learnt skills be deployed in novel contexts, using and applying mathematics, solving problems, investigating or pursuing an enquiry. The teacher's purpose will be to develop problem-solving strategies or higher levels of mathematical thinking, such as generalizing, analysis and creativity. For example, pupils having learnt how to add numbers ending in 8 or 9 using compensation might be challenged to work out how they could use a similar method for subtraction. Clearly a mismatch (overestimation) occurs if it transpires that the pupil has not mastered sufficiently the prerequisite skills that are the basis for the enrichment task. And a mismatch (underestimation) occurs if it is so obvious to the pupil how to complete the new task that no higher-level strategic skills are being developed at all.

In a perfect classroom, presumably, every task would be well matched to the child's competences and no mismatches would occur. Each child would get the intended mix of practice, incremental learning and enrichment. The findings of Bennett's team indicated, however, that in the various schools and year-groups used in their study, matching was achieved in only 30 to 40 per cent of the mathematics tasks given to pupils. Significantly, mismatching was most severe for high attainers, with, in some cases, nearly three-quarters of the tasks judged to be underestimates. Likewise, tasks given to low attainers showed a large proportion of overestimation. These results were broadly confirmed in a similar investigation undertaken in Scottish primary schools some years later (Simpson and Ure, 1994). For example, the Scottish study found that at least 50 per cent of tasks given to high attainers indicated that teachers had underestimated the pupils' ability, and that a third of the tasks that teachers gave to high attainers as enrichment tasks turned out to be no more than practice tasks for the pupils concerned. Interestingly the primary school teachers chosen for this study were all identified as being skilled at differentiation in their teaching.

PRACTICAL EXAMPLES

Typical examples of mismatch in relation to low-attaining and high-attaining pupils are given below.

Overestimating a low attainer

Overestimating the competence of low-attaining pupils is sometimes the consequence of the teacher making an assumption about understanding and mastery made on the basis of short-term success in using a recipe for a particular kind of question. For example, one low-attaining boy aged 9 years, following guidance from his teacher, completed successfully a task involving a series of questions, such as:

$$24 + 3 = \underline{} \qquad so\ 3 + 24 = \underline{}$$
$$17 + 4 = \underline{} \qquad so\ 4 + 17 = \underline{}$$

The intention here was that this would be an incremental learning task, to help the pupil to learn the mental calculation strategy of starting with the larger number in an addition and counting on by the smaller number, using his fingers. The next day the teacher quickly revised the previous day's work and the pupil was given what was intended to be a practice task, to reinforce this newly acquired learning – a worksheet, which included a number of questions such as $4 + 27$. Without the prompt of, for example, $27 + 4$, and without the repetitive pattern of the previous day's work, the pupil struggled with these additions and made numerous errors, including $3 + 39 = 69$. This is a clear example of a mismatch arising from an overestimation of what the pupil had understood, based on his apparent success in applying a recipe.

Underestimating a high attainer

With high-attaining pupils in mathematics, mismatch can sometimes occur because teachers underestimate the ability of such pupils to generalize quickly and to transfer learning from one situation to another, with the consequence that what is intended to be an enrichment task turns out to be nothing more than practice. One able 10–year-old boy

A	B
1	7
2	10
3	13
4	16
5	19
6	22

Figure 20   *What is the general rule for calculating B from A?*

was given by his teacher some number sequences to continue and, in each case, to formulate the global generalization. For example, in Figure 20, the pupil is expected to articulate that to find the number in row *B* you have to multiply the number in row *A* by 3 and add 4. The pupil wrote down the rules for these sequences immediately. When asked about this he replied: 'I've seen these before. If it's adding 3 each time it means the rule is always times by 3 plus something. If it's adding 4, you times by 4, and so on. They're easy.'

FURTHER READING

The book that provided the framework for this entry is Bennett et al. (1984). Although this work was undertaken over 20 years ago, the book is still well worth reading. Otherwise, see the suggestions for further reading in the entry for Differentiation.

RELATED ENTRIES

Differentiation. Giftedness in mathematics. Low attainment.

DEFINITION

A meaningful context is some aspect of the pupil's everyday experience in which mathematics is or can be embedded. It is a context in which pupils develop or apply their mathematics in tasks or challenges that make sense to them and in which they can be actively involved. Qualities that make a context meaningful for pupils include: the pupils know what the task is about; they can recognize a solution to a problem when it is achieved; they know when a challenge has been successfully met; they appreciate the criteria that are significant in the context concerned.

EXPLANATION AND DISCUSSION

To encourage pupils to learn mathematics meaningfully, to seek to understand their experience by making connections, rather than just to engage in rote learning of various routines and recipes, teachers in primary schools will as much as possible look for opportunities to set the mathematics in meaningful contexts.

Meaningful contexts are important for the development as well as for the application of mathematical knowledge and skills, because they promote and enhance meaningful learning. The structure of the yearly teaching programmes for the National Numeracy Strategy (DfEE, 1999b) – perpetuated in the revised National Framework (DfES, 2006a) – in which problems involving 'real life' tend to follow what appears to be the development of abstract number skills, might have inadvertently reinforced the idea in primary school teachers that this is the way in which pupils most effectively learn mathematics: first learn the skills out of any realistic context, and then learn to apply them to real-life situations and practical problems. This is not the case. Learning does not naturally proceed from the abstract to the concrete, but in the opposite direction. To introduce new mathematical concepts and skills by embedding them in meaningful contexts is to make it more likely that they will make sense to pupils. Whitebread (1995: 39) suggests that to help young children bridge the transition from informal mathematics in the context of home to the more formal mathematics of the classroom, teachers, in developing mathematical skills and concepts, should 'start with real problems, in order to present children with mathematical processes embedded in a variety of meaningful contexts'.

Haylock (1991: 65–70) demonstrates how low-attaining pupils especially benefit from mathematics that is taught through 'purposeful activities in meaningful contexts'. He provides examples of unexpected mathematical competence and commitment that can be shown by such pupils when they are engaged in tasks that have purpose and meaning. He quotes one pupil, aged about 9 years, who gained a significant insight from the challenge of working out how many containers of drinks would be needed for a (genuine) football tournament: 'You can use adding for this, Miss. I reckon that's why we learn it, so we can use it for things.' Other researchers such as Donaldson (1986), Hughes (1986) and Nunes et al. (1993) report examples of pupils across the age range of primary education who understand much better what is required of them in mathematical tasks and show a surprising grasp of some mathematical ideas when these are embedded in meaningful contexts.

The most obvious meaningful context in which mathematics can be embedded is the pupil's daily life at school, in the classroom and in the playground. Life at school involves aspects of school organization, timetables, classes, teachers and pupils. It includes the classroom routines, resources, reading books, grouping of pupils, attendance registers, rotas, layout of furniture, collecting of money, organizing events and activities, and so on. In the playground pupils need access to space, equipment and facilities. All these are contexts that are high in meaningfulness with potential for mathematical development and application. In these contexts pupils understand what counts, what is significant, what is a problem, what is a solution. Other such meaningful contexts for pupils are their daily life at home, their holiday plans, travel, sport, fund-raising, cooking, shopping, computers and entertainment (cinema, television, videos, DVDs, and so on). The more teachers can draw on such contexts in which to embed mathematical ideas and to give pupils opportunities to apply their learning, the more likely that this learning will be meaningful for them.

A highly significant part of children's lives is devoted to play, ranging across imaginative play, unstructured play and structured games. Any of these can provide a meaningful context for learning and applying mathematics. Even a purely mathematical game or puzzle has a layer of extra meaning added to it simply because it is a game and children understand what games are about and what counts as success.

PRACTICAL EXAMPLES

Four examples of the effective use of meaningful contexts in teaching mathematics are given below.

Grouping pupils in a PE lesson

A class of 28 children aged 9 to 10 years is to learn about remainders and rounding up or down in division calculations. The teacher introduces the mathematical ideas in the context of a PE lesson in the school hall, where pupils are put into groups of 4, groups of 7, groups of 5 and groups of 6 for various activities. The corresponding division statements are recorded and taken back into the classroom for discussion in a mathematics lesson.

Counting and recording sets of pupils

A class of children aged 4 to 5 years is learning to count, record and say whole numbers up to 30. Pupils in the class take turns each day to count the number of pupils present, the number absent (from the register), the number bringing packed lunches (show of hands) and the number of pupils having school meals (show of hands). The pupils report their results to the class and record the numbers on a chart.

Mathematics trail

A mathematics trail around the school's grounds or in the local area offers children opportunities to engage in a range of mathematical activities in meaningful contexts. Groups of children follow the trail, reading the questions or instructions from a prepared leaflet. Number work occurs in estimating, counting or calculating: bricks, windows, parts of playground equipment, trees. Measurement occurs in estimating and working out distances, areas, and so on. Two- and three-dimensional shapes can be found outside on the playground, or on buildings, windows and tiles. Pupils can time themselves for completing various activities, or record the time at which various observations are made. The activities can include problem solving or the collection of data for use in the classroom. Some places have published mathematics trails for use by the public: see, for example, the University of Edinburgh's maths trail along the Royal Mile (available at www.maths.ed.ac.uk/pg/trail.pdf).

meaningful context

119

Planning a class trip

A class of pupils aged 10 to 11 years is given responsibility to plan their class trip to a local castle as part of their history project. Between them various groups of pupils plan and manage every aspect of the trip, including the timetable, the programme, the costs and the transport arrangements. In doing this they apply a wide range of mathematical knowledge and skills to realistic and relevant problems in a meaningful context.

FURTHER READING

Atkinson (1992) provides examples of ways in which teachers of young children have successfully embedded mathematical processes in a range of meaningful contexts, such as playing games, sharing, birthdays, cooking, shopping, planning a picnic or a sports day, and building a nature area. Burton (1994) has a lively chapter on mathematics in a context, which is relevant to this topic. Nicol and Crespo (2005) challenge the view that meaningful contexts for learning mathematics must necessarily be realistic ones; they suggest that 'educators need to think more imaginatively about what counts as real and meaningful tasks for students' by embracing more imaginative and engaging problems.

RELATED ENTRIES

Home as a context for numeracy. Meaningful learning. Play as a context for learning mathematics. Purposeful activity.

Meaningful Learning

DEFINITION

By 'meaningful learning' we refer to a style of learning in which pupils seek not just to retain mathematical knowledge and skills in order to reproduce them later, but to actively construct meaning, by making connections between the new learning and their previous learning, by integrating the learning into their existing schemas. Meaningful learning contrasts, therefore, with rote learning.

EXPLANATION AND DISCUSSION

Mayer (2001) characterizes meaningful learning as the kind of learning in which pupils are able to use the knowledge they learn to solve problems and to understand new concepts, by transferring their knowledge to new problems and new learning situations. The concept of meaningful learning is consistent with the constructivist view of learning mathematics, where pupils are said to understand if they construct meaning from their experience by making cognitive connections between the new experiences and their previous understanding of mathematical ideas. The incoming knowledge is connected with an existing network of cognitive connections (Haylock and Cockburn, 2003: ch. 1).

Mayer (2001) identifies seven behaviours indicative of a pupil showing the kind of understanding that would count as meaningful learning, as opposed to just learning by rote These resonate strongly with the ways in which pupils in primary schools might demonstrate that they are learning mathematics in a meaningful way, as illustrated in the examples below.

Interpreting

Given the question 'How much must be added to £17.56 to make £45.06?' the pupil interprets this as a subtraction on a calculator (45.06 – 17.56) and interprets the result (27.5) as £27.50.

Exemplifying

The pupil is able to exemplify the concept of reflective symmetry by identifying in the classroom environment a number of 2-dimensional shapes with this property and the positions of the lines of symmetry.

Classifying

The pupil, having learnt about rotational symmetry, sorts a set of plane shapes into those that have rotational symmetry of order 2, order 3, order 4, and so on.

Summarizing

Having drawn a bar chart from a survey of how many pupils use various forms of transport for getting to school, the pupil writes a summary of what is shown by the graph.

Comparing

Having learnt about simple scale drawings, the pupil, given two shapes, one of which is an enlargement of the other by a factor of 2, lists all the ways in which the two shapes are the same and all the ways in which they are different.

Inferring

In an investigation about making a chain of connected squares from matchsticks, the pupil predicts how many matchsticks would be needed to make a chain of 20 squares.

Explaining

Having articulated a rule (add 3) for continuing the sequence of numbers of matchsticks required in the investigation above, the pupil explains why this rule works.

In order to make the most of pupils' experiences in mathematics lessons it is clearly important that teacher's promote meaningful learning and encourage their pupils to adopt a learning style in which they actively seek to construct meaning. Four simple ways of doing this can be suggested.

- As far as possible, set mathematics in contexts that are meaningful to pupils.
- Include activities that are specifically designed to help pupils to make connections, such as the connections between language, concrete materials, mathematical symbols and pictures.
- Plan opportunities for pupils to engage in and to be rewarded for the seven categories of behaviour indicative of meaningful learning given above.
- Model the use of mathematical language and symbols in daily classroom activities and routines. This is an approach advocated particularly for early years pupils (Tucker, 2005: 7).

PRACTICAL EXAMPLES

One geometric example and one numerical example of teachers promoting meaningful learning are provided below.

Area of a rectangle

A rote-learning approach to teaching pupils how to calculate the area of a rectangle would be to state the rule, demonstrate how to use it, rehearse it several times, and then give pupils examples to reinforce it. By contrast, a meaningful-learning approach would seek to make connections and embed the process in meaningful contexts. For example, pupils might discuss with the teacher the connection between the rectangular grids shown in Figure 21 and the three times table. They would be asked to articulate the pattern and to extend it to further examples. They would find examples of rectangular grids in the school environment and interpret these as multiplication facts. They would then be asked to draw grids on squared paper corresponding to various multiplications. Pupils would be asked to state a general rule and connections would be made with the language and notation for area. The learning would then be applied to calculating approximate areas around the classroom and in problem-solving situations, such as finding the area of a right-angled triangle.

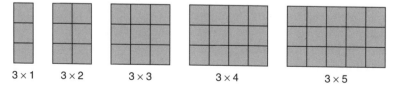

3 × 1   3 × 2   3 × 3   3 × 4   3 × 5

Figure 21   *Connecting area with the 3-times table*

Compensation in subtraction

An important calculation strategy for pupils to learn is to subtract a number ending in 8 or 9 by rounding it up to the next multiple of 10 and compensating. A teacher seeking to promote meaningful learning would ensure that pupils get the opportunity to interpret a subtraction such as 63 – 38 in a variety of ways, using a range of language, such as 'difference between', 'what must be added', and 'take away'. Then pupils would be helped by questioning to compare this subtraction with 63 – 40. Is the difference larger or smaller? Do you have to add more or add less? Do you take away more or less? Is the answer going to be larger or smaller? Pupils would make connections with pictures, such as the empty number line diagram in Figure 22, and with the manipulation of coins. They would then apply their learning to a number of examples, possibly extending to 3-digit numbers. For some examples they would be asked to provide a number line diagram and for others to write an account of how they did the calculation in a way that would explain their thinking to someone else.

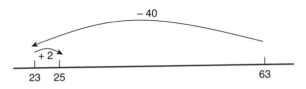

Figure 22   *An empty number line diagram connecting 63 – 38 with 63 – 40*

FURTHER READING

See the suggestions for further reading in the entry for Rote Learning. In addition, look at how Haylock and Cockburn (2003) promote the principle of making connections, particularly in chapters 1–4. A helpful summary of different perspectives on the teaching and learning of mathematics, from drill and practice theories to constructivism, is given in chapter 2 of Harries and Spooner (2000).

RELATED ENTRIES

Constructivism. Making connections. Meaningful context. Rote learning.

Mental Calculation

DEFINITION

Mental calculation in the primary school context is when a pupil manipulates the numbers involved in a calculation in their minds, using their knowledge of relationships between the numbers to operate upon them. This is instead of manipulating written symbols on a piece of paper or by using a calculator. In some cases, where they might have difficulty in remembering all the information involved in the calculation, pupils may support their mental processes by jotting down some of the numbers and intermediate results, but the essential manipulation of the numbers is still done mentally.

EXPLANATION AND DISCUSSION

In a review of research into young children engaging with powerful mathematical ideas, Perry and Dockett (2002: 93) assert that 'mental computation is an integral part of young children's learning about number' because it can contribute to children's meaningful learning of mathematical concepts and promotes 'thinking, conjecturing and generalizing based on conceptual understanding'. Mental calculations and informal methods are more likely to be based on understanding of number and numerical relationships, rather than on rote learning of routine procedures, and therefore are seen as important contributors to a pupil's 'number sense'. Confidence in mental procedures enables the pupil to deal with numerical situations in a flexible and efficient way that is determined by the numbers and operations involved.

It is this kind of conviction that led the National Numeracy Strategy (NNS) in England to place a renewed emphasis on the teaching of mental calculation strategies in primary schools. The NNS guidance (DfEE, 1999b: 6) stated that 'an ability to calculate mentally lies at the heart of numeracy'. The Numeracy Strategy recommended that teachers emphasize mental methods of calculation from the early years onwards, devoting the first 5 to 10 minutes of a numeracy lesson to mental and oral work. This policy has been reinforced in the revised National Strategy for primary schools in England, with its assertion that 'the ability to calculate mentally forms the basis of all methods of calculation and has to be maintained and refined' (DfES, 2006a: 40). This shift in emphasis in the primary mathematics curriculum towards mental calculation has put England more in line with other European countries such as the Netherlands (van den Heuvel-Panhuizen, 2001), Germany and Switzerland (Bierhoff, 1996).

The most efficient mental method for a particular calculation will depend on the numbers involved. For example, 123 – 21 will probably be done by mentally taking 21 away from 23 and then adding on the 100. However, 123 – 94 will probably be done by mentally filling the gap between the two numbers, using two steps, 6 + 23, without any actual 'taking away' involved. So teachers can help pupils to become adept at mental calculation, and therefore to develop their number sense, by providing them with a range of strategies that they can call on.

Teaching mental calculation strategies requires plenty of time for discussion and sharing of different approaches. Part of what pupils have to learn is that there is not just one right way of doing any calculation, because each person approaches a given calculation with a different set of number facts and relationships with which they are confident.

PRACTICAL EXAMPLES

Below are some examples of what the majority of pupils of various ages might reasonably be expected to manage in terms of mental calculation.

- 7-year-old pupil: calculate mentally a single-digit difference between two numbers lying either side of a multiple of 10. For example, to find 73 – 68, they might start at the 68 and mentally add on 2 to get to 70 and then 3 to get to 73, giving the difference as 5.
- 9-year-old pupil: calculate mentally the difference between any two 2-digit numbers. For example, to find 73 – 47, they might start at the 47 and mentally add on 3 to get to 50 and then a further 23 to get to 73, giving the difference as 26.
- 11-year-old pupil: calculate mentally the difference between two 4-digit multiples of 100. For example, to find 7300 – 4700, they might start at the 4700 and mentally add on 300 to get to 5000 and then a further 2300 to get to 7300, giving the difference as 2600.

In the examples above we have seen strategies such as calculating what to add on to the second number in a subtraction to reach the first number, and bridging through a multiple of 10. Below we highlight a few other strategies that might be taught specifically to primary school pupils, the prerequisite knowledge required for mental calculation, and the use of spatial imagery.

Fives and doubles

No doubt because they have two hands, with five fingers on each, and because fingers are so handy when children are learning to count, young pupils are particularly inclined to relate numbers to fives and doubles. So, for example, to calculate 5 + 7 mentally, a 5-year-old is likely to think of the 7 as 5 + 2. Then, to calculate 6 + 7 they may think of this as double 6 add 1. These are two effective strategies that can be built on for more complicated calculations. For example, pupils can be taught to reorganize 35 + 27 mentally as 35 + 25, plus 2; or to think of 36 + 37 as double 36 add 1. Older pupils can be taught to multiply mentally by 4, 8 and 16 by a process of repeatedly doubling. For example, 26 × 16 is done by doubling 26 (52), doubling the result (104), doubling again (208) and doubling again (416).

Compensation

Compensation is a strategy which is particularly useful when one of the numbers involved in a calculation is close to a number that would make the calculation very easy. For example, in 47 + 38, the 38 is close to 40, which is much easier to add on than 39. So, pupils woulds be taught to calculate mentally 47 + 40 (= 87) and then to compensate by subtracting the 2, to give the answer 85. In multiplication, a pupil at the top of the primary age range might use compensation to calculate mentally, for example, 7 × 19. Changing the 19 to 20 makes the calculation much easier (7 × 20 = 140). The compensate: because they have used 20 sevens instead of 19 sevens, one seven must be subtracted, giving the result as 133.

Friendly numbers

Extending the idea of compensation, pupils can be encouraged to look for 'friendly numbers'. For example, given 635 – 438, pupils can be asked to think of a calculation nearly the same as this but much more friendly, such as 638 – 438. The result of this is achieved very easily: 200. Then we deduce from this that 635 – 438 is 3 less than 200, namely, 197.

Using what you know

The key strategy is always to draw on what you know already to work out what you do not know. For example, knowing $2 \times 7 = 14$ enables pupils (by doubling) to work out $4 \times 7 = 28$ and $8 \times 7 = 56$, assuming they are efficient at doubling.

Prerequisite knowledge

Clearly, a prerequisite for being a good mental calculator is to have a large set of number facts (additions and multiplications, in particular) that can be recalled instantly. So, developing routine number knowledge – in a way that is based on relationships and pattern, and therefore on promoting understanding – will always be a requirement for any primary school teacher aiming to develop mental calculation skills. Other key number facts to be developed for instant recall are 10-complements (pairs of numbers that add up to 10) and, later, 100-complements (pairs of numbers that add up to 100). Additionally, pupils need to have a good grasp of the relationships between addition and subtraction, and between multiplication and division, so that they always have the option of completing a calculation involving one operation by using the inverse operation.

Spatial imagery

Finally, an important teaching principle to aid mental calculation is to provide pupils with spatial images that support mental strategies and help them to visualize the relationships between the numbers involved. The two most frequently used images are the number line in its various forms and the hundred square. (See, for example, Haylock and Cockburn, 2003: ch. 5.) Teaching pupils how to carry out simple additions and subtractions on number lines and hundred squares is therefore useful preparatory experience for doing the same calculations mentally.

FURTHER READING

Highly recommended further reading is Buys's chapter, 'Mental arithmetic' (in van den Heuvel-Panhuizen, 2001), produced by the influential TAL project in the Netherlands. Harries and Spooner (2000) is valued reading for anyone interested in both the theoretical underpinning of the teaching of mental methods and practical advice for the primary classroom. A booklet on mental calculation strategies (QCA, 1999a) was written to support the implementation of the National Numeracy Strategy. Threlfall and Frobisher, in a chapter entitled 'Patterns in processing and learning addition facts' (in Orton, 1999), provide an insightful account of how an approach to mental calculation based on pattern in number can be more successful in the long term than rote learning. Also recommended is Murray's chapter, 'Mental mathematics' (in Koshy et al., 2000).

RELATED ENTRIES

Algorithm. Informal calculation method. Skill learning.

Modelling Process (Representing)

DEFINITION

Mathematical modelling is the process whereby abstract mathematical symbols are used to represent a problem in the real world and then manipulated to find a mathematical solution, which is then used to determine an appropriate solution to the original problem back in the real world. The process can be understood as moving between the real world and the world of abstract mathematical symbols.

EXPLANATION AND DISCUSSION

The application of mathematics to real-life problems is one of the key purposes for learning the subject. In practice this usually entails setting up some kind of mathematical model, a representation of the real-life situation in mathematical symbols. For example, a problem in assessment theory is the question of how reliable is a test consisting of a number of questions. A mathematical model of this problem, using the variable r to represent a measure of reliability as a percentage (from 0 per cent, totally unreliable, to 100 per cent, totally reliable) is the formula, $r = 200c \div (1 + c)$, where c is the correlation between pupils' scores on two halves of the test. The test designer can then use this model to obtain a measure of the reliability of a test. For example, if $c = 0.25$, then the model gives the reliability as 40 per cent. If this is judged to be insufficiently high, then changes can be made to the questions and the reliability improved.

This example gives a glimpse of what mathematical modelling might look like at a more advanced level: representing a real situation in algebraic symbols, manipulating the symbols according to the rules of mathematics to obtain a mathematical solution, and then interpreting this back in the real world. English et al. (2002: 790), discussing future directions in mathematics education, suggest that the application of key mathematical ideas 'to mathematical modelling in a variety of real-world situations' is 'fundamental to success both in work environments and in life contexts in general'.

The point to be made here is that children in primary schools can begin to experience something akin to this process of modelling. English and Watters (2005: 59) suggest that research in this field supports the view that 'the primary school is the educational environment where all children should begin a meaningful development of mathematical modelling'. This is a position now endorsed in the Primary Strategy for England, which identifies 'representing' as one of the five themes in *Using and Applying Mathematics* (DfES, 2006b). Under this heading, it states (p. 7) that 'the process of selecting the key bits of information that are needed and representing the problem, using mathematical calculations, tables or diagrams, lays the foundations for the process referred to as "mathematical modelling"'. The guidance goes on to suggest (p. 8) that 'when young children correctly record tally marks to count, draw block graphs to find most frequent outcomes or use number sentences to represent some practical problem, they are beginning their journey down the road as mathematical modellers'. Using this language, Haylock (2006: ch. 4) discusses, for example, the different structures of real-life situations that might be 'modelled' by a subtraction statement (such as $12 - 7 = 5$), including inverse of addition situations (I have 7p, how much more do I need to buy something costing 12p?) and comparison situations (how much heavier is a 12-kg adult than a 7-kg child?).

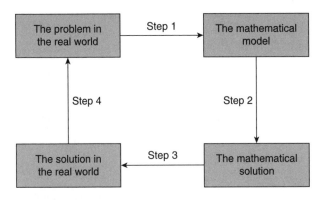

Figure 23 *A representation of the modelling process*

Figure 23 is a schematic representation of the modelling process. It starts with a problem in the real world. Step 1 is to represent this in mathematical symbols, to formulate the mathematical problem. This may involve decontextualizing the problem, extracting the essential mathematical structure from the context of the problem, detaching the numbers from the real objects, the measurements, and so on. The problem solver has now moved into the world of mathematics, 'an uncluttered and generally consistent world within which to work and think' (DfES, 2006b: 7). Step 2 is to perform the necessary calculations or other processing of the mathematical information to obtain a mathematical solution. Step 3 is to recontextualize this, to interpret the mathematical solution back in the context of the original problem. Step 4 is then to check that the solution is appropriate and that it satisfies the constraints of the original problem.

It should be emphasized that descriptions such as this are idealized and that in reality – particularly in the earlier stages of conceptual development when numbers are understood more in concrete than abstract terms – pupils will flip backwards and forwards in their thinking between the concrete embodiments of the real-world context and the abstract representation of mathematical symbols. But the importance of the modelling framework for teachers in primary schools is that it recognizes and gives value to all four of the steps involved: representing, calculating, interpreting and checking. The mathematics is not just the calculation in step 2.

PRACTICAL EXAMPLES

For example, consider what is involved when a pupil calculates the cost of 16 batteries, if they are sold at 65p for a pack of 3.

If the pupil determines that the first calculation to be done here is 16 ÷ 3 (or even 3 + 3 + 3 + 3 ... until you pass 16) to find how many packs have to be bought, they have represented one aspect of the problem in mathematical symbols. They have moved momentarily from batteries and packs to pure numbers. This is step 1 of the modelling process. Step 2 is to do the mathematical calculation, to get the result '5 remainder 1'. However, we should note that the pupil may well use a concrete embodiment of 16 ÷ 3 to enable them to do the calculation, for example, counting in 3s on their fingers until they pass 16. Step 3 is to interpret the solution '5 remainder 1' back in the real world: we need 5 packs and 1 extra battery. Step 4 is to check whether this makes sense within the constraints of the original problem: assuming you cannot actually buy a single battery, 6 packs are needed.

Then the modelling process starts again, this time to calculate the cost of 6 packs at 65p each. The mathematical representation of the problem is 65 × 6 (or, if the price is written as £0.65, the model is 0.65 × 6). This calculation might be done mentally, or by a formal written algorithm, or by pressing some buttons on a calculator. Calculating 65 × 6 mentally or by a formal written method gives the mathematical solution as 390. Doing 0.65 × 6 on a calculator the mathematical solution obtained is 3.9. To interpret either of these back in the real world (step 3), is in itself a significant piece of mathematical thinking: leading to the conclusion that the cost is £3.90. The final step is always to check the appropriateness and reasonableness of the solution. For example, if a not uncommon mistake has been made in step 3 and the solution is given as £390, a little thought about what you could buy with £390 might reveal that an error had occurred somewhere on the way!

One 10-year-old girl used 50 ÷ 12 to model the problem of how many boxes holding 12 calculators would be needed to hold a set of 50 calculators. She showed a good grasp of what step 4 in the modelling process is about when she concluded: 'You really only need 4 boxes; you can keep the extra two calculators in the drawer in the teacher's desk.'

FURTHER READING

Chapter 3 of Haylock (2006) explains more fully the modelling process as described in this entry. Subsequent chapters show how this process is involved in understanding and applying addition, subtraction, multiplication and division. For insights into the potential of upper primary pupils working collaboratively on some mathematical tasks rather closer to authentic mathematical modelling than those cited above, see 'Mathematical modelling in the primary school', a research report by English (in Putt et al., 2004). English observed a number of significant mathematical and social processes being displayed, including: interpreting and reinterpreting the given information, making appropriate decisions, justifying reasoning, posing hypotheses, and presenting arguments and counter-arguments. For similar research, examples and conclusions with younger learners, see English and Watter (2005).

RELATED ENTRIES

Making connections. Using and applying mathematics.

Numeracy

DEFINITION

A numerate person can be defined as one who can deal confidently with the numerical situations they encounter in their normal, everyday life. Confidence with numbers, including a good grasp of the relationships between them and how to operate on them in a range of practical situations and contexts, is a key characteristic of numeracy. An innumerate person will lack this confidence and may therefore be inclined to accept unquestioningly the opinions and judgements of others when numbers are involved in a transaction. It is because of its perceived importance in equipping people for the demands of living in society in a technological age that numeracy is regarded as a key goal for primary education.

EXPLANATION AND DISCUSSION

The way numeracy is understood in the above description is by no means the only way in which the concept is formulated and used. For example, different conceptions vary in terms of:

- the extent to which numeracy is understood to include aspects of mathematics other than number;
- the relative emphasis on context-free number skills or applications of number to real-life situations;
- the way in which the use of calculators is embraced.

Numeracy or mathematics?

Margaret Brown (2005: ix–x) provides a helpful analysis. She points out that in some countries numeracy is a much broader concept, something akin to mathematical literacy, and includes areas of mathematics beyond number. For example, although the Numeracy Strategy in England provided a fairly narrow definition of numeracy, as 'a proficiency which involves confidence and competence with numbers and measures' (DfEE, 1999b: 4), the framework of the strategy actually covered the whole range of mathematics content, including, for example, such topics as symmetry, classification of shapes, the coordinate system and Venn diagrams. So, in practice, following the implementation of the Numeracy Strategy, the term 'numeracy hour' replaced 'mathematics lesson' on the primary school timetable, but included teaching of number, measures, shape and space, and data handling. Significantly, the revised National Strategy for primary schools in England (DfES, 2006a), while retaining the term 'literacy', has replaced the title 'numeracy' with 'mathematics'.

Context-free skills or application?

Brown (2005) points out that the Numeracy Strategy brought with it an emphasis in the primary school curriculum on proficiency in a culturally neutral and context-free set of number skills, underpinned by abstract models such as the number line. There was limited reference in the framework to genuine applications or problem solving, other than artificial word problems. Instead, being numerate was perceived mainly as confidence and competence in a collection of numerical skills, such as knowing number facts and relationships, doubling and halving, figuring out answers mentally from what you know, calculating efficiently, mentally and on paper, and having a range of strategies for calculations. Other aspects of numeracy, such as judging whether an answer is reasonable, making sensible estimates of measurements, and interpreting numerical information presented in graphs and charts, are there, but the major emphasis is on mental and written manipulation of numbers outside any practical, realistic or meaningful context.

Askew (2001: 106) cites a functional definition of numeracy: 'The ability to process, communicate and interpret numerical information in a variety of contexts'. The idea of handling number confidently in a 'variety of contexts' is an attractive educational purpose, but it raises the question, 'Which contexts?' Most educators would say that numeracy is the ability to apply number concepts and skills to solution of problems in everyday life, employment and participation as a citizen in a democratic society. Brown (2005) points out the difficulties involved in this conception. The ways in which number is used within the social context of daily life vary markedly between different subcultures and local circumstances. For one household, being numerate might equate to being able to purchase materials for household decorations; whereas for another household it might be perceived as being able to participate intelligently in discussions about issues of national economy. Likewise, different forms of employment have varying practices and make hugely varying demands in terms of the application of numerical skills. For example, nursing would require a high level of competence in handling units of capacity such as millilitres; whereas teaching as a profession in the UK requires a high level of competence in interpreting statistical data about school performance and test results. Then, participation as an active citizen in a democratic society could involve, at one end of the scale, being able to understand and interpret bar charts in the popular press, or, at the other, being able to critique government papers on genetic modification of crops. So it is actually very difficult to agree what is the minimum competence for numeracy: whether it is just a matter of equipping individuals for social survival or something over and above this.

Calculators

Many people cope with the numerical demands they encounter in their everyday experience by using a calculator. An often quoted definition of numeracy (Girling, 1977) is the ability to use a calculator sensibly. Haylock (1991) argues that in the real world a fundamental aspect of being numerate is to know what calculation to enter on a calculator for a range of situations and to be able to interpret the answer. By contrast, for political reasons more than educational, the mathematics National Curriculum for primary schools in England (DfEE, 1999a) treated the use of calculators with some caution, effectively excluding them up to the age of 8 years, as though they were a threat to numeracy rather than a central component of it. This issue has been addressed to some extent in the new National Strategy for primary schools in England (DfES, 2006a), which, while continuing to proscribe calculators for pupils up to the age of 8 years, goes some way towards recognizing the ways in which calculators can be used by teachers to support and promote learning in mathematics.

PRACTICAL EXAMPLES

Two examples of activities promoting important aspects of numeracy are provided below.

Using a calculator to promote numeracy

An example of an effective use of calculators in a mathematics lesson demonstrates their potential for promoting numeracy. The teacher sits with a group of pupils round a table on which there is a collection of purchases with their prices clearly marked. Each pupil has a calculator. A series of questions is posed to the pupils. How much more does this cost than that? How much cheaper is this than that? How much change would I get from £10 if I bought this? How much to buy one of these and one of these? How much to buy six of these? If I have saved £2.75, how much more do I need to buy this? How many of these could I buy with £20? In each case the pupils are asked to say what they would enter on a calculator to answer the question. This focuses their attention on the mathematical structure of the problem. They then do the calculation agreed on their calculator and discuss with the teacher the interpretation of the calculator display. The activity can be repeated with similar questions in other measurement contexts, by using, for example, items marked with their mass, or containers marked with their capacity.

Large numbers

An important aspect of numeracy is the ability to make sense of relatively large numbers. Pupils might use the word 'million' freely, for example, but few would have much concept of what a set containing a million items would look like. An interesting practical project is to use a combination of photocopying, cutting and pasting, to cover a classroom wall with sheets of A3 paper containing in total a million dots. Pupils are fascinated by such big numbers and will happily engage in investigations involving practical measurement of accessible items and relating these to much larger measurements, which can be obtained from reference books or the internet. How many hamsters would weigh the same as a male African elephant? How many pupils of their age, laid end to end, would be needed to stretch from Land's End to Dunnet Head? How many glasses of water would be needed to fill a swimming pool?

FURTHER READING

Straker (in Thompson, 1999) has written a chapter entitled 'The National Numeracy Project: 1996–99', which provides insights into the approach to numeracy adopted by this influential project in England. A contrasting view is provided by Duffin (2000). She discusses the changing perceptions of numeracy in a changing world and argues the case for the integration of calculator use into the earliest years of schooling. Highly recommended is Margaret Brown's chapter, 'Effective teaching of numeracy' (in Koshy et al., 2000).

RELATED ENTRIES

Home as a context for numeracy. Meaningful context. Using and applying mathematics.

numeracy

Play as a Context for Learning Mathematics

DEFINITION

Play is a tool for learning, especially for young children. Play can take many forms and is too broad a concept to be easily defined. It is enjoyable and intrinsically motivated, often spontaneous, sometimes child initiated and child led. At other times it is structured and a collaborative endeavour between adults and children. It may be indoors, outside, at school or at home. Mathematical play can help children to begin to develop concepts in an intuitive way that they will meet more formally later on in school.

EXPLANATION AND DISCUSSION

Young children engage in play before they start formal schooling. At home, children are often involved in a playful way with day-to-day tasks, such as shopping, cooking, setting the table, gardening, as well as counting stairs and filling containers in the bath. They engage in pretend play, such as using a telephone or a toy shopping till. Many children play board games and do jigsaw puzzles at home. They therefore come to school with a variety of mathematical experiences, often gained through play. Play therefore provides a meaningful link between home and school.

In play, children can use what they know and rehearse what they are beginning to understand. They can repeat actions and develop skills at their own pace. They expand their understanding of themselves and others, their knowledge of the world around them, and their ability to communicate with children and adults.

Griffiths (2005) lists several benefits of learning mathematics through play that help children to see mathematics as enjoyable, sociable and useful in their lives:

- It has a purpose and is fun.
- It is set within a meaningful context.
- It gives the child responsibility and control.
- It provides time to repeat, practise and gain mastery.
- It is a practical activity, avoiding emphasis on written outcomes.

Tucker (2005: 6) argues that, to support mathematical development, play needs quality adult involvement at some level. This could be through planning and providing resources for stimulating learning opportunities, or through more direct involvement in the play. During play, an adult can introduce mathematical vocabulary and encourage mathematical dialogue and reasoning. Lewis (cited in Pound, 2006: 65) suggests that quality play can provide children with opportunities for making decisions, imagining, reasoning, predicting, planning, experimenting with strategies and recording. All these processes are necessary for mathematical thinking at all levels.

Practitioners frequently observe that children gain experience of all areas of learning through well-planned role play. Pretend play provides opportunities for children to learn to think abstractly, solve problems, negotiate, be imaginative, think creatively and develop social skills. Almost all Foundation Stage (3–5 years) settings and many Key Stage 1 (5–7 years) classrooms have a role-play area, which is often set up to coincide with the current topic. Role-play themes tend to fall into two broad categories of real world and fantasy (Tucker, 2005). Real-world examples would include shops (grocery, bakery, shoe shop, flower shop, and so on), café, post office, garden centre, vet, travel agents, and museum. Fantasy examples would include a rocket, a space centre, a pirate ship, a jungle, and book settings, such as Jack and the Beanstalk. All these can provide rich opportunities for mathematical learning through pretend play, although some lend themselves more successfully as contexts for mathematics than others.

Carefully chosen resources can encourage mathematical thinking and the development of mathematical skills. Resources that might be provided would include calculators, a telephone, a calendar, a diary, an appointment book, measuring equipment (balance scales, rulers, tape measures, and so on), a chequebook, a cash register, price tags, a clock, coins, stamps, and many more. Two student teachers recounted enthusiastically how they had planned an activity in the post office role-play area, which focused on wrapping up different boxes ready for posting.

They had not foreseen the amount of mathematical thinking that would occur, as the nursery children not only compared the parcels on a balance scale, but also decided how much each one would cost to post and stuck stamps on each parcel. The children also used the notepad provided to record the cost of the parcels.

Increasing importance is being placed on the value of the outdoor environment for learning and the benefits of free-flow access between the classroom and the outdoor area. An outside area provides a larger space for energetic play, which may be restricted in the classroom. Sand, water and large construction materials may well be easier to set up and use outside, where there is space and scope for more noise and mess to be acceptable. Children can explore the natural environment. The role-play area can be set up outside. There might be space for a small garden or pond. Learning to engage with mathematics in a less confined and less pressurized environment may help to make the early stages of the subject more accessible to a wider range of children.

PRACTICAL EXAMPLES

Four examples illustrate different ways of making use of play for mathematical learning.

Role-play area

In the vet's surgery there are dressing-up clothes, a variety of toy animals, weighing scales, tape measures, and thermometers. At the entrance is a notice showing the opening and closing times. The vets weigh the animals, take their temperature, examine them and prescribe medicine. X-rays are hanging up and are analysed for broken bones. The receptionist makes appointments over the phone or face to face, noting down details in the appointments book and writing out appointment cards. Bills are also settled in cash or by credit card. The children get experience of the early stages of learning to measure, sequencing of events, time of day and handling money, all in a meaningful and purposeful context.

Adult-initiated play

The teacher has noticed that the Year 1 children in the shop area tend to hand over a handful of money to pay for items and receive another handful in return (sometimes more than the amount paid!). She sets up a situation where she has dropped her purse on the floor and invites small groups of children to sort out the coins. They discuss the coins and how they could pay for items of varying costs. This leads on to the role-play area where the children and adult take turns being customer and shopkeeper.

Independent play

The children are familiar with bingo and the resources are set out on a table. A group of children play, taking turns to be the caller who takes out a numbered card and says the number to the group. As the children's number recognition develops, higher numbers can be included in the game.

Outside area

Tricycles and other toys that can be ridden are made available. Each one is numbered or has a number plate. Along the route are signposts and speed signs. There is also a postbag and a cap so the children can take turns to dress up as the postman or postwoman, and deliver letters and parcels as they ride around. The activity involves spatial concepts, including left and right, matching and numeral recognition.

FURTHER READING

A key text is Tucker (2005), which discusses the importance of play in learning mathematics and provides many practical ideas and activities. Another highly recommended book on supporting mathematics in the early years is Pound (2006). The chapter by Griffiths on 'Mathematics and play' (chapter 12 in Moyles, 2005) is also well worth reading.

RELATED ENTRIES

Home as a context for numeracy. Meaningful context. Purposeful activity

DEFINITION

A principle is a generalization that has to be learnt, remembered and applied, because it is important to the learner's understanding of the subject and their progress in learning. Mathematics in the primary school curriculum contains many important principles to be learnt.

EXPLANATION AND DISCUSSION

In Gagné's (1970) hierarchy of different categories of learning, principle learning is a higher level than concept learning, because it involves recognizing and abstracting a generalized relationship between two or more concepts.

An example of a key principle in primary school mathematics is the commutative principle of multiplication. This is a relationship that involves concepts of multiplication, order and equality. Commutativity of multiplication is the generalization that the product of two numbers is the same whichever comes first. For example, 7×5 equals 5×7. Written formally, the principle is that for any two numbers, p and q, $p \times q = q \times p$. It is clearly essential that pupils learn this principle, if they are to understand multiplication; and it is equally essential that they are able to apply it, if they are to be efficient in multiplication calculations. For example, pupils who cannot recall the result for 5 sevens will usually find it much easier if they rearrange it mentally as 7 fives. Similarly, finding the cost of 25 articles costing 16p each is most efficiently done by thinking of the calculation required as 16 twenty-fives, rather than 25 sixteens.

To enable pupils to learn a mathematical principle with understanding it is usually best for teachers to provide them with structured experiences that will lead them to articulate the principle for themselves. This will often involve the use of concrete materials or pictures that clearly model the mathematical structure of the principle. For example, to lead pupils to recognize and articulate the commutative principle for multiplication, teachers might engage pupils in investigating how many different ways 24

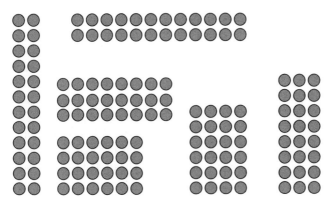

Figure 24 *In how many ways can 24 counters be arranged in a rectangular array?*

counters can be arranged in rectangular arrays, as shown in Figure 24. Through questioning, the pupils can be led to recognize that if you can have 3 rows of 8 then you can have 8 rows of 3, and so on. The principle can then be applied to other numbers of counters.

In many areas of mathematics, grasping key principles is an essential prerequisite for understanding. It is argued therefore that teachers should spend time establishing such key principles before trying to get pupils to master the routines and techniques that are underpinned by the principles.

Consider, for example, young children learning to count. The process of counting is underpinned by a number of principles, which children need to grasp (not necessarily articulate) before they can really be said to understand what counting is. Gelman and Galistel (1978) identify the following 'principles before skills' involved in counting:

- the one-to-one principle, that each object in a set must be counted just once, that is, matched with just one number tag;
- the stable order principle, that in the process of counting the number names always come in the same sequence;
- the cardinal principle, that the last number counted is the number of objects in the set;
- the abstraction principle, that the number in a set and the way you count them are independent of the qualities of the actual objects in the set;
- the order irrelevance principle, that the order in which the objects in a set are counted makes no difference (conservation of number).

principle learning

143

Piaget has identified the importance of such principles as conservation and transitivity in the child's understanding of quantity and measurement (see the separate entries for these principles). It is important that teachers of mathematics in primary schools should be aware of such principles as these underpin various mathematical processes. They will then recognize the need to provide pupils with experiences and to ask them directed questions, which are designed to promote the pupils' awareness and grasp of the principles. In this way teachers will ensure that pupils' learning of skills and processes is based on understanding and not just on learning by rote and the rehearsal of recipes and routine procedures.

PRACTICAL EXAMPLES

The commutative principle of multiplication discussed above is one of a set of key mathematical principles, which underpin all numerical calculation and which should therefore be learnt, remembered and applied by children in primary schools – not necessarily in the formal way given below, but at least articulated in informal language.

The commutative principles of addition and multiplication are:

$a + b = b + a$
$a \times b = b \times a$
for any two numbers, a and b.

These mean that the order in which two numbers are written in an addition or multiplication makes no difference to the result.

The associative principles for addition and multiplication are:

$a + (b + c) = (a + b) + c$
$a \times (b \times c) = (a \times b) \times c$
for any three numbers, a, b and c.

These mean that, if you have three numbers to add together or multiply together, it does not matter whether you start by combining the last two or the first two.

The distributive principles for multiplication and division over addition and subtraction are:

$$(a + b) \times c = (a \times c) + (b \times c)$$
$$(a - b) \times c = (a \times c) - (b \times c)$$
$$(a + b) \div c = (a \div c) + (b \div c)$$
$$(a - b) \div c = (a \div c) - (b \div c)$$
for any three numbers, a, b and c.

These four principles underpin many calculation methods for multiplication and division that break up one of the numbers into two parts. For example, the third principle listed here is used when $69 \div 3$ is changed mentally to $(60 \div 3) + (9 \div 3)$.

FURTHER READING

Bryant (in Nunes and Bryant, 1997: 54–60) provides a thorough analysis of the principles underpinning children's understanding of counting, comparing Gelman and Galistel's (1978) principles with those of Piaget. Haylock (2001: 45–56) provides further explanation and practice of the commutative, associative and distributive principles. For a discussion of the distinction between concept learning and principle learning, see the chapter by Sowder on this subject in Shumway (1980).

RELATED ENTRIES

Concept learning. Conservation of quantity. Generalization. Transitivity

problem solving

Problem Solving

DEFINITION

Many mathematical tasks involve a situation consisting of some givens and a goal. This becomes a problem for an individual if the route from the givens to the goal is not immediately obvious. Problem solving is when the individual uses their mathematical knowledge and reasoning to close the gap between the givens and the goal (Haylock, 2006: 317–18). Some problems may be purely mathematical, either numerical or spatial in content. Others may be set in real-life contexts.

EXPLANATION AND DISCUSSION

Using this definition, the following might therefore be a problem for most 11-year-olds and may be for many readers:

> Problem 1: If everyone in your class one day shakes hands with everyone else once, how many handshakes take place?

The givens are the words following 'if' up to the comma. The goal is to answer the question following the comma. But there may not be available to the person looking at this situation an immediate way of getting from the givens to the goal. A starting point here would be to clarify the givens, for example: How many people are actually in the class? A successful strategy then would be to imagine it was a very small class, say just 2 people, in which case it is easy to work out that there is just 1 handshake; or 3 people, in which case there are 3 handshakes; or 4, in which case there are 6 handshakes; and so on. The next strategy might be to tabulate these results. And so on.

Problem solving is one of the five themes in the *Using and Applying Mathematics* strand of the revised Primary Strategy in England. The guidance for this strand (DfES, 2006b: 7) states: 'Children need to solve problems to become problem solvers. Problem solving should be integrated into mathematics teaching and learning, and become a regular part of the children's work.'

Charles and Lester (1982) helpfully suggest that problem solving entails (a) actually wanting to know something, (b) lacking an obvious way to find a solution, and (c) making an effort to find the solution. If there is an obvious way to close the gap between the givens and the goal or if this can be done with no mental effort, then it is merely an exercise. For example, because some readers may have previously answered numerous questions like the handshake question above, or may even know a formula for questions like this, they might know immediately and without effort how to get from the givens to the goal. So this is for them not a problem. But Charles and Lester's first criterion is also important. If someone does not really care how many handshakes there are and has no inclination whatsoever to find out, then it is again not a problem for them. They do actually have to want to find the solution. There has to be some purpose in the problem from the pupil's perspective. This is a significant point for primary school teachers, because pupils will be motivated by different kinds of problems. For some pupils, for example, pure number puzzles will be intriguing, for others they will be pointless. Some pupils will be particularly motivated by practical problems set in real-life contexts – particularly if they are genuine problems related to their own experience, such as Problem 2 below.

Problem 2: How much should we invite each pupil to contribute for the class trip to cover our costs?

To be successful problem solvers we need strategies. There are a number of key strategies (heuristics) that can be identified for approaching mathematical problems and finding ways of solving them. In the handshake problem (Problem 1 above), for example, 'clarifying the givens' and 'starting with a simpler case' are fairly standard problem-solving heuristics.

The most influential book on solving mathematical problems was written in 1945 by George Polya (1887–1985), a Hungarian emigrant to the USA. This book continues to be a first point of reference for anyone looking at problem solving. In the second edition (1957), Polya proposed four stages in the heuristics of problem solving: understanding the problem; devising a plan; carrying out the plan; looking back. Within each of these a number of strategies used by successful problem solvers can be identified. These would include, for example: clarifying the givens; clarifying the goal; starting with a simpler problem; trial and improvement; using tabulation of a sequence of results to find a pattern or general rule; and checking whether a solution is reasonable or unique.

There is, however, little research evidence about whether or not such problem-solving strategies can be taught effectively to primary school pupils. It seems unlikely that younger pupils in the primary school will learn such strategies and then be able to deploy them in new situations, but this is not to imply that problem solving has no place in the experience of younger pupils. The Primary Strategy in England (DfES, 2006b) has objectives related to problem solving right through the primary years. The most positive outcome of a successful experience of problem solving for pupils of all ages is the satisfying sense of closure that occurs when the problem is finally solved, which gives a boost to the pupil's self-confidence and contributes to a positive attitude towards mathematics.

PRACTICAL EXAMPLES

Problem 3 below might be an appropriate challenge for Year 1 pupils, who would be able to act out with coins and objects the story involved to find the solution. This challenge would fit the problem-solving paradigm, because the pupils could have the necessary knowledge and skills but not have available an algorithm or a previously learnt procedure for finding the solution.

> Problem 3: There were four things on sale in the shop, an apple costing 5p, a pen costing 6p, a book costing 10p and a ruler costing 7p. Two of these were sold, but two of them were taken without paying! Count up how much money is in the till and work out which two things were taken without paying.

Experience suggests that teachers can help older pupils in primary schools to solve problems in mathematics by asking them questions that prompt the use of important strategies.

- What do you know? What are you told about this problem?
- Can you put this information into a picture?
- In your own words, what are you trying to find out?
- Can you think of a problem like this one that is simpler?
- Can you put these results in order in a table?
- Can you see a pattern here?
- Can you make a guess? If so, how would you know if it was right or not?
- If you are stuck, can you find another way of tackling the problem?
- Is your solution reasonable? Does it answer the question?
- Is your solution the only one possible?
- How would you explain to someone else how you solved the problem?
- Now you have solved this problem, are there other problems like this that you can think of that you could solve in a similar way?

A couple of problems will illustrate the helpfulness of asking some of these questions.

> Problem 4: In a game for two players, called Target, one player chooses a number less than 50 to be the target and the other has first turn. When it is their turn, each player chooses a number from the set {1, 2, 3, 4}, the numbers chosen being added cumulatively. The player who reaches the target is the winner. Find a strategy for winning if you have first turn, and a strategy for winning if you choose the target (provided the other player does not know the strategies as well!).

Problem 4 is a good example of a problem for older primary school pupils, because the level of reasoning involved is demanding and the solution by no means immediately apparent, but the actual arithmetic involved is very simple. The first strategy is to clarify the givens and the goal, simply by trying a few games. The teacher can then give a useful prompt by asking, 'How can you make the game really simple? Try some really small targets ... like 6 or 7 or 10'. When the problem is solved, then pupils can be asked to think how they might vary the game, by changing something (such as extending the set of numbers available up to 5, or more).

> Problem 5: There are two classes in a year group, A and B, with the same number of pupils in each class. When the bell sounds, 5 pupils move from Class A to Class B, and 13 go from Class B to Class A. Then there are twice as many pupils in Class A as there are in Class B. How many pupils are there in the year group?

Problem 5 is likely to be a problem for most of the older pupils in a primary school, because, although the numbers involved are very easy to add and subtract, there is no algorithm or obvious procedure to be applied to the numbers in the question and it involves more than one step. The teacher might encourage some key problem-solving strategies here by asking such questions as: 'Can you draw a picture to show the information you are given?' 'Can you make a guess? How would you check if your guess is right or not?' 'If your guess doesn't work, how can you make a better guess?' 'Is your answer reasonable?' 'Can you make up some more problems like this, but with different numbers, and solve them?' 'Try putting the results of all these different versions of the problem into a table and look for a pattern or a general rule.'

A couple of American books are well worth consulting, if you can get hold of them. Billstein et al. (2006) is an impressive book, now in at least its ninth edition, which promotes a problem-solving approach to mathematics in the elementary school. Baroody (1993) provides a useful summary of the problem-solving strategies that might be deployed under each of Polya's four headings, illustrating these with a range of mathematical problems. For a good supply of mathematical problems see Thyer (1993). Also recommended is Lesley Jones's thought-provoking chapter, 'The problem with problem solving' (in Thompson, 2003).

RELATED ENTRIES

Creativity in mathematics. Investigation (enquiry). Purposeful activity. Using and applying mathematics.

Purposeful Activity

DEFINITION

A purposeful activity in primary school mathematics is taken here to refer to an activity that has some kind of purpose from the pupils' perspective, sufficient to motivate them to engage with the activity with some degree of commitment to completing it.

EXPLANATION AND DISCUSSION

Teachers have their own purposes for the activities that they choose to give to pupils in mathematics lessons: to promote learning, to reinforce learning, to assess learning, to develop various kinds of mathematical thinking, and so on. Such purposes can be shared with pupils, to help them understand why they are being asked to do a particular activity.

But this does not mean that the pupils will necessarily embrace these purposes. Teachers might also consider how to make some aspects of their plans for pupils' experiences in mathematics more purposeful from the perspective of the pupil.

Ainley and Pratt (2002) argue that a common theme emerging from the constructionist (or constructivist) approach to learning mathematics (for example, Harel and Papert, 1991) and research into authentic settings for learning mathematics (for example, Nunes et al., 1993; Schliemann, 1995) is that the vital ingredients of challenge and relevance in teaching mathematics are dependent on the purposefulness of the learners' activity. 'We see this feature of purpose for the learner, within the classroom environment, as one key construct informing pedagogic task design'. They go on to define a purposeful task as 'one which has a meaningful outcome for the learner, in terms of an actual or virtual product, or the solution of an engaging problem' (Ainley and Pratt, 2002: 20).

Lave and Wenger (1991) explore the differences between 'situated learning', which is where the learning takes place in a situation for which it is actually needed, with learning in classrooms. They analysed situated learning in five different workplace settings, including midwives, tailors, and meat cutters. In all cases, knowledge and skills were gradually acquired as novices learned from experts in the context of everyday activities. A key difference between this sort of apprenticeship learning and learning in classrooms is that the outcome matters to the people doing the mathematics. There is a real purpose for learning and consequences for making mistakes, which are often absent in classroom contexts.

Of course, for many pupils in primary schools, pleasing the teacher and doing well in school are sufficient purpose to motivate them unquestioningly to do their best in the mathematical activities they are given. For some pupils, their curiosity, their natural inclination to try to understand and to discover patterns and relationships will motivate them to engage with mathematical investigations, problems and puzzles. But for many other pupils, real engagement with the tasks given to them in school mathematics requires that they perceive the tasks as having some kind of relevance to their lives.

Haylock (1991: 184–8) suggests that there are four ways in which teachers might seek to make mathematics relevant. The least effective of these in primary schools is 'long-term relevance': this is where the teacher encourages pupils to engage with some mathematics because the pupils will need it in the long term, in secondary school or in future employment. 'Vicarious relevance' is where the teacher provides pupils with problems set in real-life contexts, but they are someone else's problem, not the pupils'. This approach might achieve a degree of meaningfulness, but can still lack real purpose. There are similar shortcomings in 'artificial relevance': this is where the mathematics is set in a context that interests the pupil, such as football or television schedules, but the problems posed are not genuine problems. Ainley et al. (2005) suggest that there is considerable evidence that just setting school tasks in the context of 'real-world' situations can still fail to provide purpose from the pupil's perspective. Haylock argues for 'immediate and genuine relevance' as the key to maximizing the purposefulness of mathematical activity, particularly for low-attaining pupils. This is where the pupils use mathematics to achieve something that matters to them at the present time. Haylock calls this 'using mathematics to make things happen', and cites a number of examples of pupils showing greater commitment when engaged in activities with immediate and genuine relevance.

Ainley and Pratt (2002: 22–3) offer three reasons why a computer-based drawing task they had used successfully in their research had proved to be purposeful from the pupil's perspective: it had an explicit end product that the children cared about; it involved making something for other children; it contained opportunities for children to make meaningful decisions.

Haylock (1991: 67–70), proposing a focus on 'purposeful activities in meaningful contexts' as the key to motivating low-attaining pupils, suggests six categories of purposeful tasks that can engage pupils in using mathematics:

- solving a real problem;
- planning an event;
- design and construction;
- computer simulation;
- role play;
- games and competitions.

Not all pupils will be equally 'switched on' by all categories of activities. Some older pupils may not warm to role play, for example, and others may not have the social skills to benefit from playing small-group games. But, most primary school pupils are likely to be motivated by at least the first three categories of activity listed here. Haylock (1991: 188–9) provides the following structure for such activities, designed to maximize their purposefulness and their contribution to mathematical development.

- Identify a situation where something needs to be done that concerns the pupils.
- Give the pupils the opportunity to take responsibility for getting something done.
- Help pupils to see how they use their existing mathematical skills to help achieve their purpose.
- Take opportunities provided by the project for pupils to acquire new skills for a genuine and immediate purpose.
- Ensure that in the end mathematics is used to make something happen.
- Underline the immediate and genuine relevance of mathematics, by discussing explicitly with pupils the mathematics that was used to achieve the outcome.

PRACTICAL EXAMPLES

Below are some examples of the activities in the first three of these categories, which have been used with primary school pupils, which clearly have a high degree of purposefulness, and which have engendered impressive commitment, as well as using and developing a range of mathematic skills and knowledge.

Solving a real problem

A mixed-ability class of 10- to 11-year-olds was asked to decide the best way to arrange the furniture in the classroom for all the different activities that took place in it. The project involved: using and applying all four operations in calculations; using calculators; measurement of length; scale drawings; the concepts of area and perimeter; a range of spatial concepts; percentages; factors; and collecting, organizing, representing and interpreting data.

Planning an event

A low-attaining mathematics set of 8- to 9-year-olds was given responsibility for planning all aspects of an inter-school football tournament, normally organized by their teacher. The project, which included provision of refreshments, involved: using and applying addition, subtraction and multiplication; timetabling; spatial skills; ordering events; planning grids; a market survey; simple ratios; measurement of liquid volume and capacity; money calculations and budgeting.

Construction and design

A group of pupils aged 9 to 10 years had been learning about measurement of length in centimetres and millimetres. They were given the challenge to make a box to hold the class set of 30 calculators, with the promise that the best box would be used. The project involved: measuring lengths in centimetres and millimetres accurately; using set squares and the concept of right angles; various spatial concepts, including rectangles and cuboids; nets of a cuboid; factors; multiplication and division; concepts of perimeter, area and volume; approximation and the effect of errors in measurement.

FURTHER READING

Those who work with younger children should consult Tucker (2005) and identify some of the many examples where role play is used to provide children with opportunities to use mathematics in a way that they will perceive as purposeful. As indicated above, 'purposeful activities in a meaningful context' is one of the major themes of Haylock (1991). Lave (1988) compares the mathematics learned at school and that used in the workplace. Atkinson (1992) provides many examples of using purposeful activities with younger pupils.

RELATED ENTRIES

Low attainment. Play as a context for learning mathematics. Problem solving. Using and applying mathematics.

Questioning

DEFINITION

In this entry, questioning refers to the oral questions that teachers pose to pupils in their interactions with the class, with groups of pupils, or with individuals. Teachers ask their questions for many reasons, including: class management; assessment of learning; reinforcement of learning; and promotion of learning. In relation to the kind of learning being assessed, reinforced or promoted, questions can be classified as lower order or higher order. Questions can also be closed or open.

EXPLANATION AND DISCUSSION

Asking questions to pupils is one of the most basic and most frequently used teaching skills. Wragg and Brown (2001b: 16) report that on average teachers ask one or two questions every minute in the classroom. Good questioning skills were identified by Ofsted as one of the factors associated with high-quality teaching in primary schools in England (Oftsed, 1995). Because questioning is such a major part of the teacher's armoury it is helpful for effective teaching to be able to identify the different purposes and categories of questions that can be deployed.

First, many of the questions asked by teachers are just part of the process of class management. These would include occasions when a teacher directs a question related to the topic being taught to an individual pupil, as a means of regaining their attention. See, for example, the questions in section A below.

Second, teachers ask questions to assess learning. At the end of a teaching session, for example, teachers will ask questions to help them to determine whether or not the learning objectives for the lesson have been achieved, to check how much pupils have learnt, to assess the extent to which the concepts, principles and processes being taught have been understood or mastered. See, for example, the questions in section B below. Questions like these to assess learning will also be used at the beginning of a teaching session, when teachers check that pupils have in place the necessary knowledge and conceptual understanding that are prerequisites for the new learning. And they will be used throughout a teaching session, as teachers interact with pupils' learning by asking questions, to check that they are on track, that they understand what they are doing and that they are learning what they are supposed to be learning.

Third, teachers ask questions to reinforce learning. A mathematical process is explained and taught, but then the learning has to be reinforced through practice and rehearsal. In teaching mathematics, most primary school teachers will achieve some of this reinforcement by oral questioning. Some examples of questions used like this are given below in section C.

Fourth, teachers use questioning to promote learning. In an interactive teaching style with a class or a group, teachers' questions will help concept development. They will ask questions that stimulate pupils' curiosity and motivate them to learn. They will ask questions that promote affective as well as cognitive learning, questions designed to encourage pupils to value mathematics, to recognize its usefulness and to have a positive attitude towards it. Some examples of questions that might be asked to promote learning are given in section D below.

Of course, in practice these four purposes in questioning are not as discrete as the above analysis might suggest. Within a class, for example, a question used to reinforce learning for one pupil may prove to be a question that promotes learning for another. And every question that a teacher asks has an assessment aspect, since teachers are all the time concerned to get into their pupils' thinking and to assess whether or not they are making any sense of what is being taught.

Just as there are different levels of learning that teachers promote, reinforce and assess, so there are corresponding levels of questions. Broadly speaking, lower-order questions are related to learning knowledge of facts and mastery of skills and procedures. Such questions may elicit recall of facts, or they may engage the pupil in a mental processing of numbers, as in the questions given in Section E below. Higher-order questions are related to higher levels of learning such as understanding, application, analysis, synthesis, creativity and evaluation. They will involve fundamental mathematical processes such as forming equivalences, recognizing transformations, making generalizations, using problem-solving strategies, and thinking flexibly. Some examples are given in Section F below. Wragg and Brown (2001b: 9) report that analysis of questions asked by primary school teachers indicates that as many as 57 per cent of their questions are managerial in nature, 35 per cent are lower-order questions requiring recall of information, and only 8 per cent are higher-order questions. If these figures reflect what happens currently in mathematics lessons in primary schools it is probably fair to ask whether teachers are perpetuating a rather narrow view of the nature of mathematics, with an overemphasis on recall of facts and mastery of skills.

Questions can also be categorized as closed questions or open questions, or even half-open (Hargreaves, 1984). The clearest examples of closed questions given below are numbers 7–9 and 15–18. These elicit one, and only one, correct response. Some good examples of open questions given below are numbers 10, 13, 14, 20, 22–25. These questions allow for more than one possible response, for some exercise of judgement, for different perceptions. This distinction is important because again it reflects the teacher's understanding of the nature of learning mathematics. A teacher who sees learning mathematics in terms of knowledge and skills and routine processes will tend towards closed questions, whereas those who perceive mathematics as including an equal emphasis on problem solving, enquiry and creativity, will favour a greater proportion of open questions. The reader will no doubt have observed that, significantly, the lower-order questions in section E below tend to be closed questions, and the higher-order questions in section F tend to be open questions.

PRACTICAL EXAMPLES

A. Examples of questions used for managerial purposes

1. Jo, are you listening?
2. Mel, have you finished that graph yet?
3. Jon (who is looking out of the window), can you give us another factor of 24?

B. Examples of questions used to assess learning at the end of a teaching session

4. So, what are the three things we have to remember when drawing a bar chart?
5. Red group, how did you organize your data before you drew the bar chart?
6. Can anyone remind us why it was a good idea to do it like that?

C. Examples of reinforcement questions that a teacher might use after teaching a class the relationship between multiplication and division

7. What is 8×3? (The result is written on the board.)
8. So, if we know $8 \times 3 = 24$, what are the two division facts using these numbers that we can write down?
9. If I tell you that $154 \div 14 = 11$, what two multiplication facts could you tell me using these numbers?

D. Examples of questions promoting cognitive and affective learning

10. What do you notice is the same about all the shapes in this set?
11. Does this one belong to the set? Why not?
12. Who can guess the rule that I am using to sort these shapes?
13. Can you think of some things you could buy in the supermarket that are packaged using these shapes?
14. What was the most interesting thing that your group discovered this morning about these shapes?

E. Examples of lower-order questions requiring recall of facts or mental processes

15. How many grams in a kilogram?
16. What are 7 threes?
17. Which of 4, 8 or 12 is a factor of 28?
18. What is 27 add 5?

F. Examples of higher-order questions focused on higher levels of learning

19. So what would be a general rule for finding how many diagonals you can draw in a polygon?
20. How could we make this problem simpler to get started on it?
21. Is this shape a regular polygon? Why not?
22. If we rotate this shape through 90 degrees, like this, what has changed? What has stayed the same?
23. If we know that $24 \times 19 = 456$, what other number facts could we work out from this?
24. Which of these ways of working out 24×19 do you think is the best?
25. Which of these calculations would you do mentally? Why? Which ones would you use a calculator for? Why?

The key text on this subject is Wragg and Brown (2001b). Ainley (1987) provides an interesting perspective. She argues that the open/closed category is not as significant in mathematics teaching as the distinctions between genuine questions, questions used for control purposes, and questions of the form 'tell me what I know already' or 'guess what the teacher is thinking'. To consider the appropriate balance between lower-order and higher-order questions, read the discussion about contemporary policy issues in the teaching of mathematics provided by Reynolds and Muijs (chapter 2 in Thompson, 1999).

RELATED ENTRIES

Assessment for learning. Concept learning. Explanation. Talk.

Rote Learning

DEFINITION

Rote learning refers to a style of learning in which pupils seek only to retain and later to recall some information, result or process, without necessarily making cognitive connections between the new learning and their existing network of understanding. Rote learning contrasts, therefore, with meaningful learning.

EXPLANATION AND DISCUSSION

Mathematics, because it involves the memorization and recall of a great number of individual facts and routines, such as addition facts, multiplication tables and algorithms for calculations, is a subject that is very susceptible to rote learning. However, as Threlfall and Frobisher (1999: 65) point out, 'rote learning does not in the long term achieve the desired aim of accuracy of recall and response'. Pupils can sometimes achieve short-term success in class tests by recall of recently learnt facts and the performance of recently practised processes, but without much understanding. As a consequence the rote learning style is reinforced. Ausubel and Robinson (1969: 53–5), in their classic account of learning in schools, refer to a 'rote learning set' which can develop in pupils and which leads them to stop trying to understand and to focus only on what they have to retain and recall. In the UK, most teachers would at least claim to be committed to promoting understanding. In many countries teaching that encourages rote learning is the norm. The United Nations *Arab Human Development Report* 2004 (Farjani, 2005), for example, identifies the prevailing orthodoxy of rote learning in their schools as a major contributing factor to the lack of progress in science and research and development in some Arab countries.

Mayer (2001) notes that when teachers concentrate on rote learning, pupils are encouraged to remember fragments of knowledge in isolation from any context. Hence the knowledge being retained is unconnected to both meaningful contexts and other mathematical knowledge. For example, the pupil might be able to recall instantly that $7 \times 4 = 28$, but not connect this with $7 \times 2 = 14$ and $7 \times 8 = 56$; or be unable to describe an everyday context which would correspond to this multiplication result (such as: 'How many wheels on 7 cars, if each one has 4 wheels?'). As a consequence, the pupil is unlikely to be able to transfer the knowledge learnt by rote to new situations or practical problems. Rote learning is therefore a form of learning with limited usefulness. It is also the case that long-term retention of knowledge is more secure when pupils learn facts and processes with understanding, making connections with other mathematical knowledge and embedding the facts and processes in meaningful contexts.

Of course, it is important that pupils do memorize a considerable collection of number facts when learning mathematics in primary schools. Mayer (2001) makes the point that remembering knowledge is essential for meaningful learning and for problem solving. All higher levels of learning in mathematics, such as application, analysis, synthesis and creativity, depend upon secure and immediate access to a bank of relevant mathematical knowledge and skills. So pupils do have to memorize many things in mathematics. But it is a mistake to use 'memorizing' and 'learning by rote' as synonyms. Facts and processes can be memorized in a meaningful way, not as isolated and unconnected bits of information or routines learnt parrot-fashion, but with an emphasis on understanding.

Most of what is to be learnt in primary mathematics can be learnt meaningfully, and not just by rote, because mathematics is generally non-arbitrary and based on patterns and relationships. The patterns and relationships within the multiplication tables are a case in point. However, there are things that do just have to be learnt by rote, such as arbitrary conventions, some vocabulary and abbreviations. For example, there is a convention in algebra that x multiplied by y is written xy. There is nothing to understand here, it just has to be learnt and remembered. Learning to recite the number names from 1 to 10 is in itself a task that is simply rote learning, like learning to recite the alphabet; this is in contrast to learning to count, which involves making connections and understanding. When there are things to be learnt by rote, the learning is achieved by repetition and frequent rehearsal.

Significantly, when the material to be learnt is arbitrary and therefore low in meaning, many learners like to add artificial meaning to the material, by such things as image-association or mnemonics. For example, many pupils find it helpful to remember the arbitrary convention for coordinates, that the horizontal coordinate (x) is given first and the vertical coordinate (y) second, by associating it with the image of 'along the passage and then up the stairs'.

PRACTICAL EXAMPLES

In the primary classroom, it is important that teachers adopt a teaching style that avoids reinforcing in pupils any predilection towards a rote learning style. Classroom tests, the kinds of questions used in direct interactive teaching with the class, what kinds of responses are given the greatest rewards, for example, should all reflect a greater emphasis on learning mathematics with understanding.

There may be value in children learning to recite their multiplication tables, to aid instant recall of results. But having rehearsed, say, the 4-times table with a class of 9-year-olds, the teacher might write on the board one of the results, such as $6 \times 4 = 24$, and explore a range of connections and contexts that add meaning to this result. Pupils might be asked questions such as those given below.

- What is 4×6?
- Make up a story about shopping that uses 4×6.
- If you know $6 \times 4 = 24$, how can you work out 12×4 and 6×8?
- If you know 6×4, how can you work out 7×4?
- How many wheels on 6 cars?
- How many eggs in 4 boxes with 6 in each?

- How many sets of 6 pencils are needed to make 24 altogether?
- How many rows in a grid of 24 squares with 4 squares in each row?

In this way the teacher helps pupils to add layers of understanding to the multiplication tables and demonstrates that meaningful learning is more valued than rote learning.

FURTHER READING

Mayer's chapter, entitled 'The cognitive process dimension' (in Anderson et al., 2001), is a helpful analysis of the distinction between rote and meaningful learning that resonates well with teaching mathematics in primary schools. Chapter 3 on meaningful learning in Ausubel and Robinson (1969) is still worth reading. The reader might also evaluate their own teaching style by reference to three orientations characterizing teachers of primary mathematics (connectionist, transmission, discovery), as identified by Askew (in Thompson, 1999). The transmission orientation, which was found in the research to be only moderately effective, adopts approaches that would seem most likely to encourage a rote learning style in pupils.

RELATED ENTRIES

Algorithm. Making connections. Meaningful learning. Skill learning.

Skill Learning

DEFINITION

A skill is something that a learner learns to do with the objective being to have such a degree of proficiency that they are able to perform it repeatedly, accurately, efficiently and whenever required. Objectives for primary mathematics contain many skills, including mental and written calculation skills and the skills involved in using various mathematical devices.

EXPLANATION AND DISCUSSION

Skill learning is one of the lower levels of learning in the classic categorization of various kinds of learning provided by Gagné (1970). Compared with higher levels of learning, which would include understanding, problem solving and creative thinking, skills are relatively easy to specify as objectives and to assess. Generally speaking they are also easier to teach. Some examples of skills to be learnt in primary mathematics are:

1. counting accurately forwards and backwards in the range 0 to 100, starting from any number;
2. adding or subtracting a single-digit number to a 2-digit number by counting on or counting back mentally;
3. subtracting one 3-digit number from another using the method of decomposition;
4. using a 30-centimetre rule to draw a straight line of any length from 1 cm to 30 cm;
5. telling the time of day from an analogue 12-hour clock.

Key words in terms of mastery of skills are proficiency, accuracy, efficiency and speed. For example, in relation to skill 3 above, moving towards mastery of this skill would involve the learner becoming more proficient and accurate, so that fewer and fewer errors are made, and becoming more efficient, so that less time is spent considering what to do. In skill 4 accuracy is particularly important, but speed less so. In relation to skill 5, speed is particularly important, so that mastery of the skill is demonstrated by an almost instantaneous correct response. For each of these skills, the goal will be that pupils eventually should be able to perform the skill with very little reflection, so that the performance of the skill is effectively a reflex response exercised at a subconscious level. This means that when the learner is engaged in, say, some mathematical problem solving, they are able to call on the skills they have mastered without being distracted from the real mathematical task in front of them.

To achieve this level of mastery of skills, pupils need repetition and rehearsal, sometimes called 'drill'. All the characteristics of mastery, such as proficiency and efficiency, are improved by repeated rehearsal of the skill in question. But this takes time and there is a danger that giving a disproportionate amount of time to repetition and rehearsal of skills might give the impression that these are the essence of mathematics, rather than simply the tools required in order to engage with real mathematics and mathematical reasoning.

There is also the problem that our mastery of a skill declines if we do not use it. So, once learnt, skills need to be reinforced and refreshed. This can be achieved through simple revision of the material (the 'practice' that is usually associated with 'drill'), but the most effective way of reinforcing skills is through opportunities to use and apply them in problem-solving and mathematical investigations. They can also be used, of course, in learning new skills that build on existing skills. For example, skill 2 above clearly builds on skill 1. Careful sequencing of the programme of skills to be learnt – ensuring that pupils have in place the necessary prerequisite skills for learning each new skill – is therefore another important teaching principle.

Emphasizing aspects such as repetition, rehearsal and reinforcement might wrongly suggest that skill learning can be equated with rote learning. In a review of research into skill learning, Suydam and Dessart (1980: 208) stress that 'understanding what makes a procedure work – including the application of concepts and principles – is a necessary concomitant to skill learning'. Rittle-Johnson and Sieger (1998: 109), reviewing research into young children's learning of conceptual and procedural knowledge, conclude that 'children's understanding of mathematical concepts is positively correlated with their ability to execute procedures'.

Skemp (1977), in an influential article on pupils' understanding of mathematical processes, made a helpful distinction between 'instrumental learning', understanding what to do when faced with a particular type of mathematical question, and 'relational understanding', which is understanding why you do what you do. In terms of pupils learning number and calculation skills in primary schools, the most significant way in which relational understanding can be promoted as the basis for the skill being learnt is by making connections with appropriate language, pictures, concrete materials, such as coins and base-ten blocks, and meaningful real-life contexts.

PRACTICAL EXAMPLES

Examples of teaching approaches for skills 1 and 3 are provided below.

Skill 1

To teach counting on or back from a starting number less than 100, a teacher takes opportunities for pupils to rehearse orally the procedure with a number of examples, and reinforces this with repetition over a period of time. There is some sequencing involved, with mastery of counting on (for example, 56, 57, 58, 59, 60 ...) preceding mastery of counting back (60, 59, 58, 57, 56, ...). In counting orally, emphasis is used to underline the patterns in these processes, and hence to promote some degree of relational understanding. The teacher also makes connections between the oral recitation of the numbers and the picture of the way numbers are ordered in a hundred-square, with pupils taking turns to point to the numbers as they are counted out loud by the rest of the class.

Skill 3

To teach this skill, a teacher provides pupils with carefully sequenced examples (for example, moving from something like 53 – 37, through 453 – 237, to 403 – 237) to rehearse, develop and reinforce the procedure. But they also develop relational understanding to underpin this skill, by giving pupils opportunities to manipulate coins (1p, 10p and £1) and base-ten blocks (units, tens and hundreds) in a way that connects directly with the written calculation skill (see Haylock, 2006: 60–2). So, for example, subtracting 237 from 453 involves putting out in blocks, 4 hundreds, 5 tens and 3 units, and then experiencing how, in order to take away 7 units, one of the tens has to be exchanged for 10 units.

FURTHER READING

We suggest that you read Skemp (1977) on relational understanding and instrumental understanding, and think through how it relates to teaching mathematical skills in primary schools. Chapters 5, 6, 8 and 9 of Haylock (2006) show how mental and written calculation skills can be built on understanding, by making connections with language, pictures and concrete materials. Donlan (1998) includes a number of chapters relevant to this discussion, such as Wynn's 'Numerical competence in infants', and the Rittle-Johnson and Siegler review of conceptual and procedural knowledge quoted above.

RELATED ENTRIES

Algorithm. Making connections. Rote learning.

skill learning

DEFINITION

A feature of effective teaching of mathematics in the primary school is the teacher's planning of opportunities for pupils to engage in talking about their experiences, both with other pupils and with the teacher, and exploiting these conversations to promote and strengthen learning.

EXPLANATION AND DISCUSSION

A significant development in primary education in the UK occurred with the publication in 1975 of the influential Bullock Report (Bullock, 1975), *A Language for Life*. The specific uses of language identified by Bullock as essential experiences in schooling included, for example: reporting on present and recalled experience; collaborating towards agreed ends; and giving explanations of how and why things happen. Mathematics educators were quick to see the relevance of such ideas to the teaching of mathematics. Following the Bullock Report, the importance of pupils having opportunities to talk in mathematics lessons, both to each other and to the teacher, became established as part of what was recognized as good primary practice. The principle was enshrined in paragraph 243 of the Cockcroft Report (Cockcroft, 1982: 71), which identified, as one of six key components of good mathematics teaching, 'discussion between teachers and pupils and between pupils themselves'.

Because language plays such an important part in the development of understanding in mathematics, it follows that pupils need to be provided with opportunities to talk with their peers and with their teachers about their mathematical ideas and experiences, to share their observations, to express their questions and confusions, and to articulate their generalizations. And it is through pupils talking to them that teachers get their best insights into how much children are understanding what they are learning and what particular misunderstandings they may be carrying around. Ball (1990: 3–8) gives four reasons why a discussion-based approach to primary mathematics is beneficial.

- It improves social and personal skills, such as those necessary for working in a group, listening to others, taking turns, and giving and receiving criticism.
- It promotes better understanding, by providing pupils with opportunities to negotiate meaning from their experiences through comparing their perceptions with those of others.
- It promotes positive attitudes towards mathematics, because each pupil can feel that their contribution is valued.
- It provides assessment opportunities for the teacher, as the pupils' talk reveals misconceptions or emerging understanding.

Pupil–pupil talk can be promoted through, for example, mathematical investigations, where there may be a number of paths that might be taken or observations made, and where some negotiation between the members of the group will therefore be required. Pupils will, of course, require help in making the most of group activities. They have to be trained to work together in a way that ensures that each person in the group shares their ideas, listens to the others and compares their ideas with those of others.

Pupil–teacher talk is another key component of a discussion-based approach to teaching mathematics. In their interactions with pupils, teachers promote pupil talk most effectively through the skilful use of open-ended and challenging questions. For example, a closed question such as 'What is 6 multiplied by 4?' will promote limited pupil talk. But a follow-up open question such as 'If you know six fours make twenty-four, what other results in the multiplication tables could you work out?' could stimulate lots of pupil talk, especially if for each response the pupil is asked to explain their thinking.

The way in which a teacher responds to a pupil's contribution will be a significant factor in whether or not the pupil is inclined to speak up in future. The Mathematical Association (1987: 26) identifies as a key principle: 'The teacher must create an encouraging and receptive classroom climate'. The most effective teachers in this respect always strive to be positive and encouraging. Their pupils really believe that the teacher loves to hear their suggestions and ideas, and that answers that turn out to be wrong are just as helpful as those that are correct in helping the class to learn together.

PRACTICAL EXAMPLES

A teacher who recognizes the value of pupil talk in the development of mathematical ideas will not find it difficult to structure activities that promote discussion.

A group activity promoting pupil–pupil talk

For example, following some teaching on formal subtraction calculations using the method of decomposition, a teacher could just give pupils another sheet of examples to practise. By contrast, a teacher committed to promoting pupil–pupil talk could give groups of pupils photocopies of an imaginary pupil's work on a series of subtractions containing a number of errors and ask them to correct the pupil's work and to try to work out where the pupil has gone wrong. The group could also be asked, for the plenary, to nominate one of their members to show to the rest of the class what they think is the most interesting mistake the imaginary pupil has made.

Pooling and discussion of individual work

Pupils can engage in group investigations or group problem-solving. But equally they can work individually on tasks and then be given the opportunity to discuss their work with others. For example, pupils in a small group might individually work on how many different shapes with a perimeter of 6 cm they can draw on a square grid. Then the group can be given some time to pool their ideas, to compare each pupil's responses with those of the others, to discuss whether they are the same or different, and so on.

Teacher-led discussion

For teacher-led discussion sessions, teachers committed to encouraging pupil talk will have established the right kind of classroom ethos, in which pupils know that their ideas and contributions are welcome. They will then structure how they introduce or follow up mathematical activities accordingly. For example, in introducing a lesson on classifying three-dimensional shapes, a teacher might pass a particular solid shape round the class and ask each child to say one interesting thing about the shape, write the ideas on the board and then invite the class to discuss which are the most important attributes. Or in a plenary where pupils are sharing with the class a bar chart they have produced, the class might be asked to come up with as many different things as possible that the bar chart shows. In teaching mental calculation strategies, the teacher will automatically ask pupils to try to explain their thinking to the rest of the class. When a pupil struggles to articulate their ideas clearly, the teacher may encourage other pupils to help them out, or ask further questions to help shape the pupil's explanation.

FURTHER READING

Two helpful books are those quoted above: The Mathematical Association (1987) and Ball (1990). See also the insightful book by Brissenden (1988) on mathematical discussion in primary classrooms. There is an excellent chapter on pupil's mathematical talk in Pimm (1987). A book that brings together research on the connections between talking mathematics and learning it in school is Lampart and Blunk (1998). Higgins provides an overview of the role of talk in learning mathematics and some evidence from research in a chapter entitled 'Parlez-vous mathematics?' (in Thomson, 2003).

RELATED ENTRIES

Assessment for teaching. Language difficulties in mathematics. Making connections. Questioning.

Transformation

DEFINITION

'Transformation' is the technical mathematical term for some of the many ways in which numbers or shapes or other mathematical entities can be changed into something different by some mathematical process or other. When a transformation occurs, some attributes change, but others, sometimes very significant attributes, do not change: we say that certain 'equivalences' are preserved. So the cognitive process involved in dealing mathematically with transformations is the recognition of what changes and what stays the same. This is a fundamental component of thinking mathematically.

EXPLANATION AND DISCUSSION

In mathematics, transformations help us to analyse our observations of how things change and how they stay the same, so they are part of the process of making sense of our experiences. They are also useful mathematical tools, particularly when we can transform a shape or a number into something that is equivalent in some significant way.

Transformation in geometry

The concept of transformation is most obviously linked with geometric experience, where pupils will learn to recognize the changes that arise when shapes are subjected to transformations such as translations, rotations, reflections and enlargements, as shown in Figure 25. The National Curriculum for England (DfEE, 1999a), for example, requires that pupils at Key Stage 1 (5–7 years) should be taught to 'recognise movements in straight lines (translations) and rotation, and combine them in simple ways' (p. 65). At Key Stage 2 (7–11 years) pupils should be taught to 'transform objects in practical situations … visualise and predict the position of a shape following a rotation, reflection or translation' (p. 71). Teachers can promote pupils' awareness of transformations by asking about an object and its transformed image the key questions, 'What has changed?' and 'What is the same?' For example, in Figure 25, in transforming the shaded shape into the shape (b), all the lengths and angles in the shape are unchanged; but what has changed are the position and orientation of the shape.

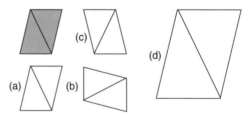

Figure 25 *Transformations of the shaded shape: (a) a translation, (b) a rotation, (c) a reflection, and (d) an enlargement.*

Transformation in measurement

The concept of transformation is related to the pupils' awareness of conservation of quantity, which is particularly significant in learning to measure. For example, to grasp the principle of conservation of volume, a pupil must recognize that if you transform the water in a jug by pouring it into another jug with a different shape, then although the height and 'shape' of the water may have changed, the volume is unchanged.

Transformation in number

In number work, pupils learn to make transformations to aid calculations. For example, in order to perform an addition or subtraction they might transform a number such as 253 into $200 + 50 + 3$. Clearly this is different from 253 (because the number has been partitioned into three bits), but pupils learn that it is also equivalent (because it represents the same quantity). Pupils may transform a subtraction such as $156 - 49$ into $157 - 50$, by adding 1 to both numbers, a transformation which leaves the difference the same. Pupils learn that you can transform a fraction by multiplying or dividing both top and bottom numbers by the same number to generate an equivalent fraction. So, for example, if they have the fraction $^6/_9$ this can be simplified to $^2/_3$ by dividing the top and the bottom numbers by 3. They also have to learn which transformations do *not* preserve certain important equivalences. For example, you do not generate an equivalent fraction by adding 3 to the top and bottom numbers ($^2/_3$ and $^5/_6$ are not equivalent fractions).

The equals sign

Interestingly, although the equals sign ($=$) is strictly used to make a statement about equivalence, pupils tend to think of it as an instruction to do something, in other words, to apply a transformation. For example, Behr et al. (1980) quote a child aged 6 years who when shown $3 + 2 = 2 + 3$ responded by saying, 'You forgot to put the 5.' So, rather than thinking of the equals sign as meaning 'is the same as' children tend to read it as 'makes'. The tendency of children to focus on the transformation rather than the equivalence when recording the results of calculations leads to a number of significant mathematical difficulties, such as a younger child giving 8 as the missing number in $\square + 3 = 5$: the equals sign says 'do something' and the addition sign tells the child what to do!

PRACTICAL EXAMPLES

To promote awareness of transformations and the equivalences that are preserved under various transformations, primary school teachers will look for opportunities for pupils to engage with examples of things being transformed by mathematical processes and then to discuss what has changed and what stays the same.

Transformation in physical education

Pupils can have practical experience of working with transformations and equivalences in physical education lessons. Two pupils stand face to face and form mirror images of each other's posture. They talk about how the two postures are the same (for example, they are both standing on one leg) and how they are different (one is standing on the right leg and one on the left leg). Two pupils stand side by side with identical posture, and then one of them turns through 90°. Or two pupils stand one in front of the other facing the same direction, with identical postures. One of them moves forward a few paces and readopts the posture. In each case they talk about how the two postures are the same and how they are different.

What counts as different?

Pupils are challenged to find how many different shapes they can make by rearranging four square tiles, recording these on squared paper. Discussion about what counts as different engages them in consideration of various ways in which shapes can be transformed, such as reflections and rotations.

Scale drawing

Pupils can make simple scale drawings of, for example, the classroom, using a scale of 1:10. They can discuss the transformation involved. Although all the lengths have been changed (reduced by a factor of 10), what has stayed the same?

FURTHER READING

Dickson et al. (1984: 51–71) provide a useful summary of children's learning about geometric transformation in the primary years. This book also has a useful summary of research related to children's understanding of the equal sign (pp. 356–8), as does Hughes (1986: 109–11). Transformation, like equivalence, is one of the central themes of Haylock

key concepts in teaching primary mathematics

and Cockburn (2003), featuring particularly in their analysis of children's learning about shape and space in chapter 7.

RELATED ENTRIES

Conservation of quantity. Equivalence.

Transitivity

DEFINITION

Transitivity is a fundamental property that may or may not be possessed by a mathematical relationship between numbers, sets, shapes or other objects. To say that a mathematical relationship is transitive means that if A is related to B and B is related to C then it follows automatically and invariably that A is related to C. Transitivity is an important property of relationships in mathematics that express equality, greater than and less than. Formally, the transitive property of equality is what seems like a very obvious assertion: if $A = B$ and $B = C$ then $A = C$. Similarly, for greater than ($>$) and less than ($<$), the transitivity properties are: if $A > B$ and $B > C$ then $A > C$; and if $A < B$ and $B < C$ then $A < C$.

EXPLANATION AND DISCUSSION

Figure 26 illustrates the defining property of a transitive relationship. For example, A, B and C could be whole numbers and the arrow might represent the relationship 'is a multiple of'. Whatever numbers are chosen, if A is a multiple of B (for example, 84 is a multiple of 42) and B is a multiple

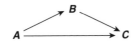

Figure 26 *The transitive property*

of C (for example, 42 is a multiple of 7), then it follows that *A* must be a multiple of C (it is: 84 is a multiple of 7). The fact that this always works makes the relationship 'is a multiple of' a transitive one.

Not all relationships are transitive. For example, in geometry, two ways of relating straight lines are by the concepts of 'parallel' and 'perpendicular' (at right angles to). The relationship 'is parallel to' is clearly transitive. But the relationship 'is perpendicular' is not. If line *p* is at right angles to line *q* and line *q* is at right angles to line *r*, then *p* is not necessarily at right angles to *r*. It could be, as you can see where three lines meet in a corner of a room. But it is not *necessarily* the case, for example, if *p*, *q* and *r* are three sides of a square.

In terms of primary school children learning mathematics, the most significant experiences of transitivity are in relationships of measurement. For example, to use a balance and one 100-g mass to make a set of 100-g masses from play-dough is to employ the principle that if *A* weighs the same as *B* and *B* weighs the same as C then *A* weighs the same as C. So, if *A* is 100 g and *B* is an equal mass, then if *B* balances a pile of sand (C) then this is 100 g of sand. Comparative relationships, such as 'longer than', 'heavier than' and 'holds more than', are the basis of the reasoning used to put objects in order according to attributes such as length, weight and capacity. In getting to grips with this principle, children learn, for example, that if John is taller than Meg and Meg is taller than Sean, then John must be taller than Sean. If the jar holds less than the jug and the jug holds less than the bottle, then the jar must hold less than the bottle. If the book is heavier than the calculator and the calculator is heavier than the pencil case, then the book must be heavier than the pencil case. Applying this principle repeatedly, children are able to put in order sets of objects from smallest to largest in terms of their lengths, their heights, their capacities, their weights, and so on.

The ability to make transitive inferences – along with the principle of conservation of quantity – was identified by the educational psychologist, Jean Piaget, as one of the key indicators of the development of children's understanding. Testing individual children on various tasks related to transitivity (see, for example, Inhelder and Piaget, 1964) he concluded that most children grasped the principle of transitivity in length and weight around the age of 8 years. Piaget's developmental model was that children could apply the principle of transitivity once they had matured sufficiently to infer the consequence of *A* > *B* and *B* > C by logical reasoning. This position was subsequently challenged by other researchers, who demonstrated that applying the principle relies on other factors such as memory and perception (Bryant and Trabasso, 1971; Duncan and McFarland, 1980).

Some researchers have shown how children younger than 8 years can apply the transitivity principle successfully in a practical context that makes sense to them. In practice, any problem involving reasoning based on an intervening measure requires a grasp of this principle. Bryant and Kopytynska (1976) gave such a problem to children aged 5 and 6 years. Two blocks of wood had small holes drilled in them and the children were challenged to find out which hole was deeper. The children had access to a measuring stick with marks on, which would fit into the holes. The children were for the most part successful in deducing which was the deeper hole from their observations of what happened when they put the stick in the holes. To do this they demonstrated the ability to grasp the relationship between the depths of the holes without making a direct comparison between them; in other words, they made transitive inferences.

PRACTICAL EXAMPLES

Primary school teachers should recognize that the principle of transitivity lies at the heart of children's experiences of comparing three or more quantities or measurements and putting them in order from smallest to largest, or from largest to smallest. Any experience of putting sets of three or more objects in order according to some measurement attribute will therefore give children experience of this principle.

Transitivity in comparing capacities

For example, having compared pairs of containers to decide which holds more and which holds less, children should move on to put a set of three containers in order from the one that holds the least to the one that holds the most. This can be done before the introduction of units of capacity (litres and millilitres). Including tall containers with relatively small capacities and shorter containers with relatively large capacity may make it more likely that the logic of the transitivity principle at the heart of the ordering process, rather than just perception, will come into play in the child's completion of the task.

Transitivity in weighing

Similarly, in learning about weight, pupils will start by directly comparing two objects to decide which is heavier and which is lighter, using a balance. From this they should move on to putting sets of three or more objects in order from lightest to heaviest, or from heaviest to lightest, by successively using the balance to compare one with another. Again, including large objects that are relatively light in weight and smaller objects that are relatively heavy may make it more likely that the pupil will use the logic of the transitivity principle, which lies at the heart of this ordering process.

FURTHER READING

Nunes and Bryant (1996: ch. 4) provide a helpful summary of the cognitive processes that underpin children's thinking about measurement, including transitivity. Haylock and Cockburn (2003: ch. 6) discuss the mathematics of transitivity and ordering in measurement contexts. Smith et al. (2003: ch. 12), provide a thorough and interesting account of Piaget's theory of children's development, including the significance of transitive inferences. Readers interested in Piaget's theories and their implications for teaching and learning will find it helpful to refer to chapters 1–3 of Wood (1998).

RELATED ENTRIES

Conservation of quantity. Principle learning.

Using and Applying Mathematics

DEFINITION

'Using and applying mathematics' is the first attainment target in the English National Curriculum (DfEE, 1999a). This has three strands:

learning to solve problems both in real life and within mathematics itself; developing skills of communication using mathematical language and symbols; and developing the ability to reason in a mathematical way. In the review of the primary framework (DfES, 2006b), 'Using and applying mathematics' is one of seven core areas of learning mathematics, now presented with five themes: solving problems, representing, enquiring, reasoning, and communicating.

EXPLANATION AND DISCUSSION

Mathematics in primary schools is not just about knowledge of facts and conventions, mastery of skills and understanding of mathematical concepts. Pupils must also learn to use and to apply their knowledge, skills and concepts to some purpose. It is for this reason that 'Using and applying mathematics' has always featured prominently in the English National Curriculum for mathematics. One of the four attainment targets in the version of the National Curriculum for mathematics that became statutory in 2000 is devoted to using and applying mathematics, suggesting that it might constitute 25 per cent of what pupils should achieve. Each section of the programmes of study (Number; Shape, Space and Measures; Handling Data) begins with a set of teaching targets for using and applying the mathematical content of that section. For Number at Key Stage 1 (5–7 years), what pupils should be taught includes to 'make decisions about which operations and problem-solving strategies to use' and to 'present results in an organised way' (DfEE, 1999a: 62). For Number at Key Stage 2 (7–11 years), they should be taught to 'find different ways of approaching a problem in order to overcome any difficulties' and to 'organise work and refine ways of recording' (DfEE, 1999a: 67).

However, in practice, many primary school teachers in England did not use this National Curriculum document as the basis for designing their teaching programmes and instead relied on the Framework for the National Numeracy Strategy (DfEE, 1999b). Hughes et al. (1999: 69) have argued that this framework shifted the emphasis towards number knowledge and calculation skills, with only one of the 13 key objectives for Year 2 and only one of the 11 key objectives at Year 4 relating to the application of numeracy.

- Year 2: Choose and use appropriate operations and efficient calculation strategies to solve problems, explaining how the problem was solved.

- Year 4: Choose and use appropriate number operations and ways of calculating (mental, mental with jottings, pencil and paper) to solve problems.

There has therefore been some potential for primary school teachers to lose sight of the significance and importance of their pupils learning to use and to apply their mathematical knowledge and skills. Mathematics is, after all, of little use to us if we cannot take what we learn in one context and apply it to other contexts. Context-free number skills, such as being able to divide 450 by 12, are of no value at all if we cannot call on them appropriately in real-life situations, such as when calculating how many rows of 12 chairs would be required to seat an audience of 450 people. The revised National Framework for primary schools in England (DfES, 2006a, 2006b) has recognized this shift in emphasis away from using and applying mathematics outlined above and has gone some way towards ensuring that this aspect of mathematics is more firmly embedded in the primary school curriculum. For Year 2, for example, five of the 27 objectives for mathematics are directly linked to the National Curriculum's 'Using and applying mathematics' attainment target; and for Year 4, the proportion is five out of 32.

Hughes et al. (2000) provide evidence that both children and adults have difficulty in applying mathematical knowledge acquired in one context to problems posed in another. Their research suggests that teachers and curriculum designers underestimate the complexities involved in the transfer of existing mathematical learning to new situations. Teachers should recognize the varying demands involved in transferring mathematical skills and knowledge to different contexts and new problems. Sometimes the transfer is fairly straightforward, because the similarities between the two situations are strong enough for pupils to see the connections. Other times there can be a significant cognitive distance between the two contexts and transfer can be challenging. In these cases, without appropriate teaching, many pupils will not apply their mathematical knowledge but will look on the new situation as providing a completely different set of things to learn. Some examples below illustrate these ideas.

PRACTICAL EXAMPLES

Some pupils have been learning to calculate differences between two 2-digit numbers, using a hundred-square, by adding on, making explicit use of the multiples of 10 at the ends of the rows.

1. The teacher gives them the opportunity to apply the process they have learnt, by bridging through multiples of 10 on a number line to calculate differences. This could be an example of using and applying mathematics, but there is a strong possibility that many pupils will not see the connections between the two different contexts and regard them as two different kinds of mathematical questions. The teacher must be alert to this possibility and use questioning to help pupils with this.
2. Next, the pupils apply the same process to finding differences between distances measured in centimetres on a 100-cm rule. The transfer of learning involved here from the number line examples is less challenging because of the strong contextual similarities.
3. The teacher provides a number of purchases priced in pence, up to £1, and pupils use coins to calculate the differences in costs between various pairs of items. The distance between this context and the original hundred-square context would be considerable, even though the underlying mathematical processes are the same. Again it is likely that many pupils will need help in making explicit the relationship between the contexts, so that the problems with the coins become an application of their earlier learning, not just another new process to learn.
4. Having experienced the same process in four different contexts, pupils may now be constructing their own understanding of how to calculate the difference between two numbers. This can then be applied to various number puzzles or challenges, such as; (a) find two 2-digit numbers that differ by 28, given that one of them begins with a 3 and the other ends in a 3; (b) how many different pairs of 2-digit numbers have a difference of 79?
5. The skills learnt can also be applied to problems set in real-life contexts. These could be artificial word problems (for example, John is 25 and his Dad is 52. What is the age difference?). Or they could be genuine real-life contexts, such as doing a survey of the difference in age between the mother and the oldest child in the families of the children in the class.
6. Finally, the calculation skills learnt here might be just some of the mathematics that is drawn on later in a real problem-solving experience, such as pupils planning their own timetable for a day at school.

FURTHER READING

Hughes et al. (2000) provide an insightful analysis of the problems of transferring mathematical learning to new situations, with some interesting accounts of primary school teachers taking different approaches to the application of mathematics. Sellars and Lowndes have provided two books on this subject (2002a, 2002b), one for each of Key Stages 1 and 2. Both books provide advice on how pupils can be taught strategies to enable their thinking skills to progress and to develop different approaches to problem solving, with plenty of practical suggestions for classroom activities. As part of its review of the National Strategy for primary schools, the DfES has produced specific guidance, *Using and Applying Mathematics* (DfES, 2006b).

RELATED ENTRIES

Investigation (enquiry). Meaningful context. Modelling process (representing). Problem solving.

References

Adey, P. and Shayer, M. (1990) 'Accelerating the development of formal thinking in middle and high school students', *Journal of Research in Science Teaching*, 27(3): 267–85.

Adey, P., Robertson, A. and Venville, G. (2002) 'Effects of a cognitive acceleration programme on Year 1 pupils', *British Journal of Educational Psychology*, 72: 1–25.

Ainley, J. (1987) 'Telling questions', *Mathematics Teaching*, 118: 24–7.

Ainley, J. and Pratt, D. (2002) 'Purpose and utility in pedagogic task design', in A. Cockburn and E. Nardi (eds), *Proceedings of the 26th Annual Conference of the International Group for the Psychology of Mathematics Education*. Norwich: University of East Anglia.

Ainley, J., Bills, L. and Wilson, K. (2005) 'Purposeful task design and the emergence of transparency', in H. Chick and J. Vincent (eds), *Proceedings of the 29th Annual Conference of the International Group for the Psychology of Mathematics Education*. Melbourne: University of Melbourne.

Ambrose, R., Baek, J. and Carpenter, T. (2003) 'Children's invention of multidigit multiplication and division algorithms', in A. Baroody and A. Dowker (eds), *The Development of Arithmetic Concepts and Skills: Constructing Adaptive Expertise*. Mahwah, NJ: Lawrence Erlbaum Associates.

Anderson, L., Krathwohl, D., Airasian, P., Cruikshank, K., Mayer, R., Pintrich, P., Raths J. and Wittrock, M. (2001) *A Taxonomy for Learning, Teaching, and Assessing: A Revision of Bloom's Taxonomy of Educational Objectives*. New York: Longman.

Ashcraft, M. and Kirk, E. (2001) 'The relationships among working memory, math anxiety, and performance', *Journal of Experimental Psychology*, 130(2): 224–37.

Ashcraft, M., Kirk, E. and Hopko, D. (1998) 'On the cognitive consequences of mathematics anxiety', in C. Donlan (ed.), *The Development of Mathematical Skills*. Hove: Psychology Press.

Askew, M. (1999) 'It ain't (just) what you do: effective teachers of numeracy', in I. Thompson (ed.), *Issues in Teaching Numeracy in Schools*. Buckingham: Open University Press.

Askew, M. (2001) 'Policy, practices and principles in teaching numeracy: what makes a difference?', in P. Gates (ed.), *Issues in Mathematics Teaching*. London: RoutledgeFalmer.

Assessment Reform Group (1999) *Assessment for Learning: Beyond the Black Box*. Cambridge: University of Cambridge School of Education.

Assessment Reform Group (2002) *Assessment for Learning, 10 Principles: Research-Based Principles to Guide Classroom Practice*. Cambridge: Assessment Reform Group.

Atkinson, S. (ed.) (1992) *Mathematics with Reason*. London: Hodder and Stoughton.

Ausubel, D. and Robinson, F. (1969) *School Learning: An Introduction to Educational Psychology*. New York: Holt, Rinehart and Winston.

Ball, G., with the Lakatos Primary Mathematics Group (1990) *Talking and Learning: Primary Maths for the National Curriculum.* Oxford: Blackwell.

Baroody, A. (1993) *Problem Solving, Reasoning, and Communicating, K–8: Helping Children Think Mathematically.* New York: Macmillan.

Baroody, A. and Dowker, A. (eds) (2003) *The Development of Arithmetic Concepts and Skills: Constructing Adaptive Expertise.* Mahwah, NJ: Lawrence Erlbaum Associates.

Behr, M., Erlwanger, S. and Nichols, E. (1980) 'How children view the equals sign', *Mathematics Teaching*, 92: 13–15.

Bennett, N., Desforges, C., Cockburn, A. and Wilkinson, B. (1984) *The Quality of Pupil Learning Experiences.* London: Lawrence Erlbaum Associates.

Bierhoff, H. (1996) *Laying the Foundations for Numeracy.* London: Economic and Social Research Council.

Billstein, R., Libeskind, S. and Lott, J. (2006) *A Problem Solving Approach to Mathematics for Elementary School Teachers.* 9th edn. Boston, MA: Addison Wesley.

Black, P. (2003) *Assessment for Learning: Putting it into Practice.* Maidenhead: Open University Press.

Boero, P., Douek, N. and Ferrari, P. (2002) 'Developing mastery of natural language: approaches in theoretical aspects of mathematics', in L. English (ed.), *Handbook of International Research in Mathematics Education.* Mahwah, NJ: Lawrence Erlbaum Associates.

Briggs, M. (2003) *Assessment for Learning and Teaching in Primary Schools.* Exeter: Learning Matters.

Brissenden, T. (1988) *Talking About Mathematics: Mathematical Discussion in Primary Classrooms.* Oxford: Blackwell.

Brown, M. (2000) 'Effective teaching of numeracy', in V. Koshy, P. Ernest and R. Casey (eds), *Mathematics for Primary Teachers.* London: Routledge.

Brown, M. (2001) 'Influences on the teaching of number in England', in J. Anghileri (ed.), *Principles and Practices in Arithmetic Teaching: Innovative Approaches for the Primary Classroom.* Buckingham: Open University Press.

Brown, M. (2005) 'Foreword', in B. Street, D. Baker and A. Tomlin, *Navigating Numeracies: Home/School Numeracy Practices.* Dordrecht: Springer.

Browne, A. and Haylock, D. (eds) (2004) *Professional Issues for Primary Teachers.* London: Sage Publications.

Bryant, P. (1997) 'Mathematical understanding in the nursery school years', in T. Nunes and P. Bryant (eds), *Learning and Teaching Mathematics: An International Perspective.* Hove: Psychology Press.

Bryant, P. and Kopytynska, H. (1976) 'Spontaneous measurement by young children', *Nature*, 260: 773.

Bryant, P. and Trabasso, T. (1971) 'Transitive inferences and memory in young children', *Nature*, 232: 456–8.

Bullock, A. (1975) *A Language for Life.* London: HMSO.

Burnett, S. and Wichman, A. (1997) *Mathematics and Literature: An Approach to Success.* Chicago, IL: Saint Xavier University and IRI/Skylight.

Burton, L. (1984) *Thinking Things Through: Problem Solving in Mathematics.* Oxford: Blackwell.

Burton, L. (1994) *Children Learning Mathematics: Patterns and Relationships.* Oxford: Blackwell.

Buxton, L. (1991) *Math Panic.* London: Heinemann Educational Books.

Buys, K. (2001) 'Mental arithmetic', in M. van den Heuvel-Panhuizen (ed.), *Children Learn Mathematics: A Learning-Teaching Trajectory with Intermediate Attainment Targets for Calculation with Whole Numbers in Primary School.* Groningen: Wolters-Noordhoff.

Carpenter, T. and Lehrer, R. (1999) 'Teaching and learning mathematics with understanding', in E. Fennema and T. Romberg (eds), *Mathematics Classrooms that Promote Understanding.* Mahwah, NJ: Lawrence Erlbaum Associates.

Carruthers, E. and Worthington, M. (2006) *Children's Mathematics: Making Marks, Making Meaning.* 2nd edn. London: Paul Chapman Publishing.

Charles, R. and Lester, F. (1982) *Teaching Problem-Solving: What, Why and How.* Paolo Alto, CA: Dale Seymour Publications.

Child, D. (2007) *Psychology and the Teacher.* 8th edn. London: Continuum.

Clarke. S. and Atkinson, S. (1996) *Tracking Significant Achievement in Primary Mathematics.* London: Hodder and Stoughton.

Clements D. and Sarama J. (eds) (2004) *Engaging Young Children in Mathematics: Standards for Early Childhood Mathematics Education.* Mahwah, NJ: Lawrence Erlbaum Associates.

Cockburn, A. (1999) *Teaching Mathematics with Insight: The Identification, Diagnosis and Remediation of Young Children's Mathematical Errors.* London: Falmer Press.

Cockburn, A. (ed.) (2007) *Mathematical Understanding 5–11.* London: Sage Publications.

Cockcroft W. (Chairman) (1982) *Mathematics Counts: Report of the Committee of Inquiry into the Teaching of Mathematics in Schools.* London: HMSO.

De Geest, E., Watson, A. and Prestage, S. (2002) 'Building a holistic view of mathematical thinking: data evaluation of improving attainment in mathematics project', *Proceedings of the British Society for Research into Learning Mathematics*, 22(3): 19–24.

Department for Education and Employment (DfEE) (1999a) *The National Curriculum: Handbook for Primary Teachers in England.* London: DfEE and QCA.

Department for Education and Employment (DfEE) (1999b) *The National Numeracy Strategy: Framework for Teaching Mathematics from Reception to Year 6.* London: DfEE.

Department for Education and Employment (DfEE) (2000) *National Literacy and Numeracy Strategies: Guidance on Teaching Able Children.* London: DfEE.

Department for Education and Skills (DfES) (2001) *Guidance to Support Pupils with Dyslexia and Dyscalculia.* London: DfES.

Department for Education and Skills (DfES) (2003) *Excellence and Enjoyment: A Strategy for Primary Schools.* London: DfES.

Department for Education and Skills (DfES) (2005) *Supporting Children with Gaps in their Mathematical Understanding.* London: DfES.

Department for Education and Skills (DfES) (2006a) *The Primary Framework for Literacy and Mathematics: Core Position Papers Underpinning the Renewal of Guidance for Teaching Literacy and Mathematics.* London: DfES.

Department for Education and Skills (DfES) (2006b) *Reviewing the Primary Framework for Mathematics, Guidance Paper: Using and Applying Mathematics.* London: DfES.

Dickson, L., Brown, M. and Gibson, O. (1984) *Children Learning Mathematics: A Teacher's Guide to Recent Research.* London: Cassell.

Dienes, Z. (1963) *An Experimental Study of Mathematics Learning.* London: Hutchinson.

Donaldson, M. (1986) *Children's Minds.* London: HarperCollins.

Donlan, C. (ed.) (1998) *The Development of Mathematical Skills.* Hove: Psychology Press.

Dowker, A. (2004) *What Works for Children with Mathematical Difficulties? (DfES Research Report 554).* London: DfES.

Drews, D. (2005) 'Children's mathematical errors and misconceptions: perspectives on the teacher's role', in A. Hansen (ed.), *Children's Errors in Mathematics: Understanding Common Misconceptions in Primary Schools.* Exeter: Learning Matters.

Duffin, J. (2000) 'We must not let the future be the prisoner of yesterday's ideas', *Teaching Mathematics and its Applications,* 19(2): 56–61.

Duncan, E. and McFarland, C. (1980) 'Isolating the effects of symbolic distance and semantic congruity in comparative judgments: an additive-factors analysis', *Memory and Cognition,* 8: 612–22.

Edwards, S. (1998) *Managing the Effective Teaching of Mathematics 3–8.* London: Paul Chapman Publishing.

English, L. (2004) 'Mathematical modelling in the primary school', in I. Putt, R. Faragher and M. McLean (eds), *Proceedings of the 27th Annual Conference of the Mathematics Education Research Group of Australasia. Mathematics Education for the Third Millennium: Towards 2010.* Townsville: James Cook University.

English, L. and Watters, J. (2005) 'Mathematical modelling in the early school years', *Mathematics Education Research Journal,* 16(3): 58–79.

English, L., Jones, G., Lesh, R., Tirosh, D. and Bussi, M. (2002) 'Future issues and directions in international mathematics education research', in L. English (ed.), *Handbook of International Research in Mathematics Education.* Mahwah, NJ: Lawrence Erlbaum Associates.

Ernest, P. (1991) *The Philosophy of Mathematics Education.* London: Falmer Press.

Ernest, P. (2000) 'Why teach mathematics?', in J. White and S. Bramall (eds), *Why Learn Maths?* London: London University Institute of Education.

Farjani, N. (2005) *The Arab Human Development Report 2004, Towards Freedom in the Arab World.* New York: United Nations Development Programme 2005.

Ford, S., Staples, P., Sheffield, D. and Valnono, L. (2005) 'Effects of maths anxiety on performance and serial recall', paper presented at the British Psychological Society Annual Conference 2005, 30 March to 2 April, Manchester.

Freeman, J. (2003) 'Gender differences in gifted achievement in Britain and the US', *Gifted Child Quarterly,* 47(3): 202–11.

Freudenthal, H. (1973) *Mathematics as an Educational Task.* Dordrecht: D. Reidel Publishing.

Frobisher, L. and Threlfall, J. (1999) 'Teaching and assessing patterns in number in the primary years', in A. Orton (ed.), *Pattern in the Teaching and Learning of Mathematics*. London: Cassell.

Fuson, K. (2004) 'Pre-K to Grade 2 goals and standards: achieving 21st century mastery for all', in D. Clements and J. Sarama (eds), *Engaging Young Children in Mathematics: Standards for Early Childhood Mathematics Education*. Mahwah, NJ: Lawrence Erlbaum Associates.

Gagné, R. (1970) *The Conditions of Learning.* 2nd edn. New York: Holt, Rinehart and Winston.

Gallagher, A. and Kaufman, J (eds) (2005) *Gender Differences in Mathematics: an Integrative Psychological Approach.* Cambridge: Cambridge University Press.

Gardner, H. (2000) *Intelligence Reframed: Multiple Intelligences for the 21st Century.* New York: Basic Books.

Gates, P. (ed.) (2001) *Issues in Mathematics Teaching.* London: RoutledgeFalmer.

Gelman, R. and Galistel, C. (1978) *The Child's Understanding of Number.* Cambridge, MA: Harvard University Press.

Gifford, S. (2005) *Teaching Mathematics 3–5: Developing Learning in the Foundation Stage.* Maidenhead: Open University Press.

Girling, M. (1977) 'Towards a definition of basic numeracy', *Mathematics Teaching,* 81: 4–5, 13–14.

Goulding, M. (1997) *Learning to Teach Mathematics.* London: David Fulton.

Grant, F. (1996) 'The calculator-based laboratory and distance–time graphs', *Micromath,* 12(3): 16–17.

Grauberg, E. (1998) *Elementary Mathematics and Language Difficulties: A Book for Teachers, Therapists and Parents.* London: Whurr Publishers.

Griffiths, R. (2005) 'Mathematics and play', in J. Moyles (ed.), *The Excellence of Play.* 2nd edn. Maidenhead: Open University Press.

Gura, P. (1992) *Exploring Learning: Young Children and Blockplay.* London: Paul Chapman Publishing.

Hafeez, R. (2003) 'Using assessment to improve teaching and learning', in I. Thompson (ed.), *Enhancing Primary Mathematics Teaching.* Maidenhead: Open University Press.

Hanna, G. (ed.) (1996) *Towards Gender Equity in Mathematics: An ICMI study.* Dordrecht: Kluwer Academic.

Hansen A. (ed.) (2005) *Children's Errors in Mathematics: Understanding Common Misconceptions in Primary Schools.* Exeter: Learning Matters.

Harel, I. and Papert, S. (1991) *Constructionism.* Norwood, NJ: Ablex.

Hargreaves, D. (1984) 'Teachers questions: open, closed, and half-open', *Educational Research,* 26(1): 46–51.

Harries, T. (2001) 'Working through complexity: an experience of developing mathematical thinking through the use of Logo with low attaining pupils', *Support for Learning,* 16(1): 17–22.

Harries, T. and Spooner, M. (2000) *Mental Mathematics for the Numeracy Hour.* London: David Fulton.

Haylock, D. (1984) *'Aspects of mathematical creativity in children aged 11–12'.* Unpublished PhD thesis, University of London.

Haylock, D. (1986) 'Mathematical low attainers checklist', *British Journal of Educational Psychology*, 56: 205–8.

Haylock, D. (1991) *Teaching Mathematics to Low Attainers, 8–12*. London: Paul Chapman Publishing.

Haylock, D. (2001) *Numeracy for Teaching*. London: Paul Chapman Publishing.

Haylock, D. (2004) 'Gifted and talented pupils in primary schools', in A. Browne and D. Haylock (eds), *Professional Issues for Primary Teachers*. London: Sage Publications.

Haylock, D. (2006) *Mathematics Explained for Primary Teachers*. 3rd edn. London: Sage Publications.

Haylock, D. and Cockburn, A. (2003) *Understanding Mathematics in the Lower Primary Years*. 2nd edn. London: Paul Chapman Publishing.

Haylock, D., Blake, G. and Platt, J. (1985) 'Using maths to make things happen', *Mathematics in School*, 14(2): 32–4.

Headington, R. (2000) *Monitoring, Assessment, Recording, Reporting and Accountability: Meeting the Standards*. London: David Fulton.

Hejny, M. and Slezáková, J. (2007) 'Investigating mathematical reasoning and decision making', in A. Cockburn (ed.), *Mathematical Understanding 5–11*. London: Sage Publications.

Henderson A., Came F. and Brough M. (2003) *Working with Dyscalculia*. Marlborough: Learning Works International.

Hiebert, J. and Carpenter T. (1992) 'Learning and teaching with understanding', in D. Grouws (ed.), *Handbook of Research on Mathematics Teaching and Learning*. New York: Macmillan.

Hiebert, J., Carpenter, T., Fennema, E., Fuson, K., Wearne, D., Murray, H., Oliver, A. and Human, P. (1997) *Making Sense: Teaching and Learning Mathematics with Understanding*. Portsmouth, NH: Heinemann.

Higgins, S. (2003) 'Parlez-vous mathematics?', in I. Thompson (ed.), *Enhancing Primary Mathematics Teaching*. Maidenhead: Open University Press.

Houssart, J. (2004) *Low Attainers in Primary Mathematics*. London: RoutledgeFalmer.

Hughes, M. (1986) *Children and Number*. Oxford: Blackwell.

Hughes, M., Desforges, C. and Mitchell, C. (1999) 'Using and applying mathematics at Key Stage 1', in I. Thompson (ed.), *Issues in Teaching Numeracy in Primary Schools*. Buckingham: Open University Press.

Hughes, M., Desforges, C. and Mitchell, C., with Carré, C. (2000) *Numeracy and Beyond: Applying Mathematics in the Primary School*. Buckingham: Open University Press.

Inhelder, B. and Piaget, J. (1964) *The Early Growth of Logic in the Child: Classification and Seriation*. London: Routledge and Kegan Paul.

Jaworski, B. (2003) 'Inquiry as a pervasive pedagogic process in mathematics education development', in M.A. Mariotti, *Proceedings of CERME3 (Third International Conference of the European Society for Research in Mathematics Education)*. Bellaria: ERME.

Joffe, L. and Foxman, D. (1986) 'Attitudes and differences: some APU findings', in L. Burton (ed.), *Girls into Maths Can Go*. London: Cassell.

key concepts in teaching primary mathematics

Jones, L. (2003) 'The problem with problem solving', in I. Thompson (ed.), *Enhancing Primary Mathematics Teaching*. Maidenhead: Open University Press.

Jones, L. and Allebone, B. (2000) 'Differentiation', in V. Koshy, P. Ernest and R. Casey (eds), *Mathematics for Primary Teachers*. London: Routledge.

Kaltman, G. (2005) *More Help! for Teachers of Young Children: 99 Tips to Promote Intellectual Development and Creativity*. London: Sage Publications.

Kennard, R. (2001) *Teaching Mathematically Able Children*. 2nd edn. London: David Fulton, in association with NACE.

Koshy, V. (2000a) *Teaching Mathematics to Able Children*. London: David Fulton.

Koshy, V. (2000b) 'Children's mistakes and misconceptions', in V. Koshy, P. Ernest and R. Casey (eds), *Mathematics for Primary Teachers*. London: Routledge.

Koshy, V., Ernest, P. and Casey, R. (eds) (2000) *Mathematics for Primary Teachers*. London: Routledge.

Krutetskii, V. (1976) *The Psychology of Mathematical Ability in Schoolchildren*. Eds, J. Kilpatrick and I. Wirzsup. Tr. J. Teller. Chicago, IL: University of Chicago Press.

Lampart, M. and Blunk, M. (1998) *Talking Mathematics in School*. Cambridge: Cambridge University Press.

Lave, J. (1988) *Cognition in Practice: Mind, Mathematics, and Culture in Everyday Life*. Cambridge: Cambridge University Press.

Lave, J., and Wenger, E. (1991) *Situated Learning: Legitimate Peripheral Participation*. Cambridge: Cambridge University Press.

Liebeck, P. (1990) *How Children Learn Mathematics: A Guide for Parents and Teachers*. London: Penguin.

Mayer, R. (2001) 'The cognitive process dimension', in L. Anderson, D. Krathwohl, P. Airasian, K. Cruikshank, R. Mayer, P. Pintrich, J. Raths and M. Wittrock, *A Taxonomy for Learning, Teaching, and Assessing: A Revision of Bloom's Taxonomy of Educational Objectives*. New York: Longman.

McGarrigle, J. and Donaldson, M. (1974) 'Conservation accidents', *Cognition*, 3: 341–50.

Merttens, R. (1996) *Teaching Numeracy: Maths in the Primary Classroom*. Leamington Spa: Scholastic.

Merttens, R. (1999) 'Family numeracy', in I. Thompson (ed.), *Issues in Teaching Numeracy in Primary Schools*. Buckingham: Open University Press.

Merttens, R. and Vass, J. (eds) (1993) *Partnership in Maths: Parents and Schools – the Impact Project*. London: RoutledgeFalmer.

Moyles, J. (ed.) (2005) *The Excellence of Play*. 2nd edn. Maidenhead: Open University Press.

Murray, J. (2000) 'Mental mathematics', in V. Koshy, P. Ernest and R. Casey (eds), *Mathematics for Primary Teachers*. London: Routledge.

National Advisory Committee on Creative and Cultural Education (NACCCE) (1999) *All Our Futures: Creativity, Culture and Education*. London: DfES.

National Council for Teachers of Mathematics (NCTM) (1995) *Connecting Mathematics Across the Curriculum* (1995 Yearbook). Reston, VA: NCTM.

Nelson, D., Joseph, G. and Williams, J. (1993) *Multicultural Mathematics: Teaching Mathematics from a Global Perspective*. New York: Oxford University Press.

Nicol, C. and Crespo, S. (2005) 'Exploring mathematics in imaginative places: rethinking what counts as meaningful contexts for learning mathematics', *School Science and Mathematics*, 105(5): 240–2.

Niss, M. (1993a) 'Assessment in mathematics education and its effects: an introduction', in M. Niss (ed.), *Investigations into Assessment in Mathematics Education: An ICMI Study*. Dordrecht: Kluwer Academic.

Niss M. (ed.) (1993b) *Investigations into Assessment in Mathematics Education: An ICMI Study*. Dordrecht: Kluwer Academic.

Nunes, T. and Bryant, P. (1996) *Children Doing Mathematics*. Oxford: Blackwell.

Nunes, T. and Bryant, P. (eds) (1997) *Learning and Teaching Mathematics: An International Perspective*. Hove: Psychology Press.

Nunes, T., Schliemann, A. and Carraher, D. (1993) *Street Mathematics and School Mathematics*. Cambridge: Cambridge University Press.

Nutbrown, C. (2006) *Key Concepts in Early Childhood Education and Care*. London: Sage Publications.

Office for Standards in Education (Ofsted) (1995) *Teaching Quality: The Primary Debate*. London: Ofsted.

Office for Standards in Education (Ofsted) (2003) *The National Literacy and Numeracy Strategies and the Primary Curriculum*. London: Ofsted.

Office for Standards in Education (Ofsted) (2005) 'Mathematics in primary schools', *The Annual Report of Her Majesty's Chief Inspector of Schools, 2004/05*. London: Ofsted.

Orton, A. (ed.) (1999) *Pattern in the Teaching and Learning of Mathematics*. London: Cassell.

Orton, A. (2004) *Learning Mathematics: Issues, Theory and Classroom Practice*. 3rd edn. London: Continuum.

Orton, A. and Orton, J. (1999) 'Pattern and the approach to algebra', in A. Orton (ed.), *Pattern in the Teaching and Learning of Mathematics*. London: Cassell.

Page G. and Thomas, J. (1979) *International Dictionary of Education*. London: Kogan Page.

Perry, B. and Dockett, S. (2002) 'Young children's access to powerful mathematical ideas', in L. English (ed.), *Handbook of International Research in Mathematics Education*. Mahwah, NJ: Lawrence Erlbaum Associates.

Piaget, J. (1952) *The Child's Conception of Number*. London: Routledge and Kegan Paul.

Piaget, J. (1953) *The Origin of Intelligence in the Child*. London: Routledge and Kegan Paul.

Piaget, J. (1977) *The Development of Thought: Equilibration of Cognitive Structures*. New York: Viking Press.

Piaget, J. and Inhelder, B. (1972) *The Child's Construction of Quantities: Conservation and Atomism*. London: Routledge and Kegan Paul.

Pimm, D. (1987) *Speaking Mathematically: Communication in Mathematics Classrooms*. London: Routledge and Kegan Paul.

Pinker, S. (1998) *How the Mind Works*. London: Penguin.

Pirie, S. and Kieran, T. (1992) 'Creating constructivist environments and constructing creative mathematics', *Educational Studies in Mathematics*, 23: 505–28.

Polya, G. (1957) *How to Solve It.* 2nd edn. Princeton, NJ: Princeton University Press.

Pomerantz, E., Altermatt, E. and Saxon, J. (2002) 'Making the grade but feeling distressed: gender differences in academic performance and internal distress', *Journal of Educational Psychology*, 94(2): 396–404.

Porter, L. (2005) *Gifted Young Children: A Guide for Teachers and Parents.* 2nd edn. Maidenhead: Open University Press.

Pound, L. (2006) *Supporting Mathematical Development in the Early Years.* 2nd edn. Maidenhead: Open University Press.

Putt, I., Faragher, R. and McLean, M. (2004) (eds) *Proceedings of the 27th Annual Conference of the Mathematics Education Research Group of Australasia. Mathematics Education for the Third Millennium: Towards 2010.* Townsville: James Cook University.

Qualifications and Curriculum Authority (QCA) (1997) *Standards at Key Stage 2, English Mathematics and Science: Report on the 1997 National Curriculum Assessments for 11-year-olds.* London: QCA.

Qualifications and Curriculum Authority (QCA) (1999a) *Teaching Mental Calculation Strategies: Guidance for Teachers at Key Stages 1 and 2.* London: QCA, for the National Numeracy Strategy.

Qualifications and Curriculum Authority (QCA) (1999b) *Teaching Written Calculation Methods: Guidance for Teachers at Key Stages 1 and 2.* London: QCA, for the National Numeracy Strategy.

Resnick, L. (1982) 'Syntax and semantics in learning to subtract', in T. Carpenter, J. Moser and T. Romberg (eds) *Addition and Subtraction: A Cognitive Perspective.* Englewood Cliffs, NJ: Laurence Erlbaum Associates.

Reynolds, D. and Muijs, D. (1999) 'Numeracy matters: contemporary policy issues in the teaching of mathematics', in I. Thompson (ed.), *Issues in Teaching Numeracy in Primary Schools.* Buckingham: Open University Press.

Rittle-Johnson, B. and Siegler, R. (1998) 'The relationship between conceptual and procedural knowledge in learning mathematics', in C. Donlan (ed.), *The Development of Mathematical Skills.* Hove: Psychology Press.

Schliemann, A. (1995) 'Some concerns about bringing everyday mathematics to mathematics education', in L. Meira and D. Carraher (eds), *Proceedings of the 19th Conference of the International Group for the Psychology of Mathematics Education.* Recife: PME.

Sellars, E. and Lowndes, S. (2002a) *Using and Applying Mathematics at Key Stage 1: A Guide to Teaching Problem Solving and Thinking Skills.* London: David Fulton, in association with NACE.

Sellars, E. and Lowndes, S. (2002b) *Using and Applying Mathematics at Key Stage 2: A Guide to Teaching Problem Solving and Thinking Skills.* London: David Fulton, in association with NACE.

Shumway, R. (ed.) (1980) *Research in Mathematics Education.* Reston, VA: National Council of Teachers of Mathematics.

Simpson, M. and Ure, J. (1994) *Studies of Differentiation Practices in Primary and Secondary Schools (Interchange 30).* Edinburgh: Research and Intelligence Unit, Scottish Council for Research in Education.

Skemp, R. (1993) *The Psychology of Learning Mathematics.* 2nd edn. London: Penguin. (1st edn. 1971.)

references

Skemp, R. (1977) 'Relational understanding and instrumental understanding', *Mathematics Teaching*, 77: 20–6.

Smith, P., Cowie, H. and Blades, M. (2003) *Understanding Children's Development.* 4th edn. Oxford: Blackwell.

Soro, R. (2002) 'Teachers' beliefs about gender differences in mathematics: "girls or boys?" scale', in A. Cockburn and E. Nardi (eds), *Proceedings of the 26th Annual Conference of the International Group for the Psychology of Mathematics Education.* Norwich: University of East Anglia.

Sowder, L. (1980) 'Concept and principle learning', in R. Shumway (ed.), *Research in Mathematics Education.* Reston, VA: National Council of Teachers of Mathematics.

Straker, A. (1999) 'The National Numeracy Project: 1996–99', in I. Thompson (ed.), *Issues in Teaching Numeracy in Primary Schools.* Buckingham: Open University Press.

Street, B., Baker, D. and Tomlin, A. (2005) *Navigating Numeracies: Home/School Numeracy Practices.* Dordrecht: Springer.

Suydam, M. and Dessart, D. (1980) 'Skill learning', in R. Shumway (ed.), *Research in Mathematics Education.* Reston, VA: National Council of Teachers of Mathematics.

Swetz, F. and Kao, T. (1977) *Was Pythagoras Chinese? An Examination of Right Triangle Theory in Ancient China.* Reston, VA: National Council of Teachers of Mathematics and Pennsylvania State University Press.

Thangata, F. (2004) 'Education for a multicultural society', in A. Browne and D. Haylock (eds), *Professional Issues for Primary Teachers.* London: Sage Publications.

The Mathematical Association (1987) *Maths Talk.* Cheltenham: Stanley Thornes.

Thompson, I. (ed.) (1997) *Teaching and Learning Early Number.* Buckingham: Open University Press.

Thompson I. (ed.) (1999) *Issues in Teaching Numeracy in Schools.* Buckingham: Open University Press.

Thompson, I. (ed.) (2003) *Enhancing Primary Mathematics Teaching.* Maidenhead: Open University Press.

Threlfall, J. (1999) 'Repeating patterns in the early primary years', in A. Orton (ed.), *Pattern in the Teaching and Learning of Mathematics.* London: Cassell.

Threlfall, J. and Frobisher, L. (1999) 'Patterns in processing and learning addition facts', in A. Orton (ed.), *Pattern in the Teaching and Learning of Mathematics.* London: Cassell.

Thyer, D. (1993) *Mathematical Enrichment Exercises: A Teacher's Guide.* London: Cassell.

Tomlinson, C. (2000) 'Reconcilable differences? Standards-based teaching and differentiation', *Educational Leadership*, 58(1): 6–11.

Torrance, E. (1966) *Torrance Tests of Creative Thinking: Norms Technical Manual.* Princeton, NJ: Personnel Press.

Treffers, A., Nooteboom, A. and de Goeij, E. (2001) 'Column calculation and algorithms', in M. van den Heuvel-Panhuizen (ed.), *Children Learn Mathematics: A Learning-Teaching Trajectory with Intermediate Attainment Targets for Calculation with Whole Numbers in Primary School.* Groningen: Wolters-Noordhoff.

Tucker, K. (2005) *Mathematics Through Play in the Early Years: Activities and Ideas.* London: Paul Chapman Publishing.

Turner, S. and McCullough, J. (2004) *Making Connections in Primary Mathematics.* London: David Fulton.

Van den Heuvel-Panhuizen, M. (ed.) (2001) *Children Learn Mathematics: A Learning-Teaching Trajectory with Intermediate Attainment Targets for Calculation with Whole Numbers in Primary School.* Groningen: Wolters-Noordhoff.

Verschaffel, L. and De Corte, E. (1997) 'Word problems: a vehicle for promoting authentic mathematical understanding and problem solving in the primary school?', in T. Nunes and D. Bryant (eds), *Learning and Teaching Mathematics: An International Perspective.* Hove: Psychology Press.

Von Glaserfeld, E. (1995) *Radical Constructivism.* London: Falmer Press.

Vygotsky, L. (1978) *Mind in Society.* Cambridge, MA: Harvard University Press.

Watson, A. (2000) 'Going across the grain: mathematical generalisations in a group of low attainers', *Nordic Studies in Mathematics Education,* 8(1): 7–20.

Weston, P., Taylor, M., Lewis, G. and MacDonald, A. (1998) *Learning from Differentiation: A Review of Practice in Primary and Secondary Schools.* Slough: NFER.

White, J. and Bramall, S. (eds) (2000) *Why Learn Maths?* London: London University Institute of Education.

Whitebread, D. (1995) 'Emergent mathematics or how to help young children become confident mathematicians', in J. Anghileri (ed.) *Children's Mathematical Thinking in the Primary Years: Perspectives on Children's Learning.* London: Cassell.

Wigley, A. (1997) 'Approaching number through language', in I. Thompson (ed.), *Teaching and Learning Early Number.* Buckingham: Open University Press.

Williams, E. and Shuard, H. (1994) *Primary Mathematics Today.* 4th edn. Harlow: Longman.

Wood, D. (1998) *How Children Think and Learn.* 2nd edn. Oxford: Blackwell.

Wragg, E. (ed.) (1984) *Classroom Teaching Skills.* London: Croom Helm.

Wragg, E. and Brown, G. (2001a) *Explaining in the Primary School.* Rev edn. London: RoutledgeFalmer.

Wragg, E. and Brown, G. (2001b) *Questioning in the Primary School.* Rev edn. London: RoutledgeFalmer.

Wright, R., Martland, J. and Stafford, A. (2005) *Early Numeracy: Assessment for Teaching and Intervention.* 2nd edn. London: Paul Chapman Publishing.

Wynn, K. (1998) 'Numerical competence in infants', in C. Donlan (ed.), *The Development of Mathematical Skills.* Hove: Psychology Press.

Zaslavsky, C. (1996) *The Multicultural Math Classroom: Bringing in the World.* Portsmouth, NH: Heinemann.

references